PRAISE FOR VINCENT GREEN'S
EXTREME JUSTICE

"EXTREME JUSTICE is history that reads like the best legal thrillers. This is one of the last untold stories of World War II—it demands to be read."

—Gerry Spence, *New York Times* bestselling author of *How to Argue and Win Every Time*

"EXTREME JUSTICE is a f—————— k which combines excellent hi——————————n, legal intricacies, an

—Prof—————————————iversity, autho

"Powerful, mov—————————JSTICE* is vivid narrative hist————— a human scale, an unflinching examination of the dark side of military justice, and, as Green demonstrates, a parable of and for our brutal times."

—George Garrett, author of *Death of the Fox*

"EXTREME JUSTICE is a gripping account of a fascinating and troubling murder case. Vincent Green has the literary and legal skill to make both the German POWs' actions and the American Army lawyers' tactics come to life."

—John Casey, winner of the 1989 National Book Award for *Spartina*

"Great history. . . . *EXTREME JUSTICE* reads like a classic Clancy novel but unfortunately it's true. Brilliant."

—Colonel David H. Hackworth, USA (Ret.), *New York Times* bestselling author of *About Face: The Odyssey of an American Warrior*

DID THESE MEN SERVE JUSTICE . . . OR EXACT REVENGE?

Corporal Johannes Kunze—A forty-year-old infantryman in bad health, he hated his Nazi leaders as much as he loved the idea of America. Captured and shipped to a POW camp in Oklahoma, he traded highly sensitive information—that would lead to many German deaths—for the promise of a new life in California. But betrayal was answered with betrayal, and Corporal Kunze paid with his life.

First Sergeant Walter Beyer—A member of the once-vaunted Afrika Korps under Rommel, he knew even before he was taken prisoner that the homeland was bound for defeat. Yet in captivity, he lived by a military code of honor, faith, and loyalty—a code that he would never break, up to the day he marched down death row to the Fort Leavenworth gallows.

Lieutenant Colonel Leon Jaworski—In civilian life, the small, intense thirty-eight-year-old Texas lawyer had already established himself as one of the best litigators in the country. Taking over the prosecution of the five German POWs, Jaworski seized the opportunity to prove just how devastating he could be in a military courtroom.

Lieutenant Colonel Alfred Petsch—Assigned to defend Walter Beyer, Petsch was a simple old country lawyer with minimal experience in criminal cases. At trial, his counterpart, Leon Jaworski, would demonstrate just how out-classed and ill-equipped Petsch was to handle the defense.

Staff Sergeant Berthold Seidel—A second defendant in the case, Seidel was a large, striking soldier with battlefield experience in North Africa and on the Russian front. His toughness and candor, however, would prove disastrous to the defense and would give Jaworski a critical edge in the prosecution.

Werner Weingaertner—A Swiss diplomat attending the trial as an observer, Weingaertner expressed concerns about the harshness of the verdict and sentence. His was a voice of reason—but amid horrid reports of the German concentration camps, it was a voice that no one wanted to hear.

Books by Vincent Green

FICTION
The Price of Victory

NONFICTION
Extreme Justice

EXTREME JUSTICE

VINCENT GREEN

POCKET BOOKS

New York   London   Toronto   Sydney   Tokyo   Singapore

An *Original* Publication of POCKET BOOKS

POCKET BOOKS, a division of Simon & Schuster Inc.
1230 Avenue of the Americas, New York, NY 10020

ISBN: 0-671-79906-1

First Pocket Books printing October 1995

10 9 8 7 6 5 4 3 2 1

POCKET and colophon are registered trademarks of
Simon & Schuster Inc.

Cover photo courtesy of the author; inset photo courtesy of the
U.S. Army.

Printed in the U.S.A.

FOR CHRIS

Acknowledgments

This book could not have been written without the help of many people. In Germany I would like to thank Edgar and Marianne Beyer for showering me with unexpected hospitality as well as information about Walter Beyer and Hamburg. Freddie Bergmann arranged interviews and contacted people with information. Dr. Tristan Rolfs acted as an interpreter (every writer should be able to take along a psychiatrist on interviews). Kurt Trummel and Achilles Rehberger provided information about the Tonkawa POW Camp.

In America I would like to thank Steve Ward for his research at the National Archives and Truman Library. John Reichley at Leavenworth, Kansas gave me great leads on this story. Rex Ackerson and the Oklahoma Historical Society in Tonkawa provided background on the POW camp and photos. Silke Sjolie was a great help in translating letters and documents from German to English. Ed Green saved time by obtaining and taking photos.

Additionally, the following books provided invaluable background material: *The Killing of Corporal Kunze* by Wilma Parnell: *Martial Justice* by Richard Whittingham; *Nazi POWs in America* by Arnold Krammer; *Truman* by David McCullough; *Confession and Avoidance* by Leon Jaworski.

I would like to thank Peter Rubie and Paul McCarthy for their editing. You're the best!

Finally, to my wife, Chris, and daughters, Molly and Maggie, thanks for your love and patience.

Author's Note

Some of the witnesses to these events are dead or could not be located. I have taken the liberty to fill in their thoughts and beliefs and to re-create their conversations, where I thought it was appropriate and warranted by court records, documents, letters and conversations with individuals who witnessed the events.

Extreme justice is often injustice.

—*Cicero*

1

Defeat in the Desert

Tunisia
April 1943

HAUPTFELDWEBEL WALTER BEYER SCANNED THE SOUTH-
ern horizon with his binoculars, waiting for the Stukas and BF 110 *Zerstrores* to return to the airfield
outside Mejez el Bab. Fifty kilometers away reddish
brown dust rose off the desert shelf and hovered like
bad air over a polluted city. Tanks! Thousands of
Shermans and Grants were pushing closer every day,
tightening the noose. The British and Americans
would soon drive what was left of the Afrika Korps
into the Mediterranean. Beyer had already seen the
signs.

Less than a week ago a general and his entourage
had arrived for an inspection. They swept in from
Panzerführer Headquarters in Tunis—fancy staff cars,
gold-braided uniforms, scarves rakishly tied around
their necks. The general was fat and wore a leather
overcoat like Rommel's; his girth made him waddle
like a pregnant cow. He had stopped and talked to
several of Beyer's men, inquired about families and

1

mail, and slapped each man on the back while he laughed too heartily. Before he left, the general had read a letter from the Führer, who exhorted the Afrika Korps to hold fast to the last man and promised "a glorious triumph," led by Rommel himself, back into Egypt, taking Alexandria and Cairo. All lies—the clearest sign of all the end was near.

With one hand, Beyer swatted flies away from his lips so he could concentrate. The heat was horrendous and produced its own misery. Beyer felt the burning itch of prickly heat on his back and chest, and resisted the urge to scratch it raw. There was barely enough water to drink, so no one had bathed in months. A man sweated in the same uniform day after day until it was ready to rot off his back, and as a result, they all smelled worse than camels. The terrible odor of your comrades (you soon learned to ignore your own smell so you didn't go crazy) was the unexpected torture of the war in the desert. Beyer had grown to relish his moments alone, away from the other men.

Finally, eight dots appeared on the horizon. Beyer watched as the V-shaped formation came clearly into view, checking for the Iron Cross on the fuselage. Definitely eight. Damn it. They had sent off ten planes this morning.

"Children," Beyer yelled. He always called his men children as a sign of affection, especially when he was worried. "Up. Hurry, here they come."

His ground crew of twenty men piled out of the tents covered with camouflaged netting and sandbagged bunkers, and rushed to the fuel tanks and bomb racks. Their days had been like this since January. Nonstop bombing missions. Planes lost every day to the superior numbers of Hurricanes and P-40s. Always the pressure to put up as many planes as possible, with no replacement parts. Cannibalizing three planes to make one run. The ground crews had nicknamed themselves "blackmen," and now that the end seemed near, all the men joked about being one of the lost tribes of Africa, abandoned here, wandering the desert in vain until the end of the war.

Beyer panned his binoculars toward the west and saw two long tendrils of smoke arching up in the bright blue sky. He prayed they were burning enemy tanks; knew they were probably planes—their planes. No time to mourn. In the past year he'd learned that lesson, too.

The planes circled: the Stukas first followed by the twin-tailed fighters, lining up their approach by sighting off the date palms near the end of the strip. The planes seemed to float down out of the sky like hawks gliding for the kill, talons extended, cutting their engines as they neared the strip, then reversing the thrust the minute the wheels set down to brake. Each plane kicked up a succeedingly larger cloud of dust off the dirt runway.

By the time all the planes landed, Beyer stood in a dust storm. He pulled his Pith helmet down over his eyes and turned his back as the planes taxied closer to the fuel drums. The sand stung the bare skin below his shorts as the pilots revved the engines once more before shutting down.

Two crews began pushing 50-liter fuel drums and hydraulic pumps closer so they could fill wingtanks. Another crew struggled to move a bomb dolly through the sand toward the belly of a Stuka. Beyer jumped in and lent his back to the action, and the bomb started to move. As a teen Beyer had been weak and scrawny, but he had grown into a tall, strong man. Handsome, too, with sharp wolfish features, thick bushy eyebrows, dark brown hair, and blue eyes.

He'd spent nine years in the Luftwaffe—Germany, Sicily, now Tunisia. It was not the life he had intended, but he had little choice. For a short time in Hamburg he had been a draftsman's apprentice, but then the economy bottomed out. He could still remember the days his mother took wheelbarrows full of deutsche marks to the bakery just to buy a loaf of bread, and the day his supervisor told him he was a good worker, but they had no money to pay him anymore. So he'd become a professional soldier. In many ways he wasn't cut out for military life. Early on, he'd been court-martialed twice for sneaking away to see his future wife, Edith. He didn't drink, and some of the men resented that. Despite all this he had risen in rank, and the men who worked for him feared his quick temper and obeyed his every order.

After much pushing, Beyer and his men finally aligned the bomb under the Stuka, attached a pulley, then leveraged the bomb into the rack. Beyer jumped out of the way as his men connected the fuse and he raced to oversee the refueling of one of the BF-110s. The pilot pulled back the canopy and slid his goggles up on his leather flight cap. He perched himself on his seat and lit a cigarette, affecting the nonchalant attitude of a veteran pilot, even though he was barely nineteen and in his first month of combat. The pilot was so new to the squadron that Beyer had trouble remembering his name. In some ways that made sending him on missions easier, especially if he didn't make it back. Beyer handed him a canteen.

Beyer asked, "What about Sauer and Helbig?" Sauer was the best pilot in the squadron; he had received the Knights Cross for his thirtieth air kill. It seemed inconceivable he'd been lost.

The young pilot shook his head sadly, then gave a thumbs down. "A wall of steel," he said, gesturing back to the south. He drank greedily from the canteen, tipping it to find the last drops of water, then tossed it back to Beyer. "Soon we will be marching into Cairo. What do you think, First Sergeant, two weeks at the most?"

Such a boy, thought Beyer, all studied indifference and swagger to hide his fear. Beyer smiled at the black humor. "Then on to England the week after that."

Before he buttoned the canopy, the pilot yelled to Beyer. "Be alert, Tommies are everywhere."

As soon as the blackmen had the planes in the air, Beyer ordered Sergeant Baade to form a detail and haul the empty fuel drums to the storage dump near the village mosque. The backwash from the planes' landing had a tendency to blow empty drums onto the landing strip and slow the refueling process.

Beyer watched as his men efficiently hauled ammunition and bombs into place for the next mission, then carefully covered them with camouflage netting. A lookout was posted with the flak gunner to keep watch for enemy planes, so Beyer sat down on an upturned ammunition box to take a breather. As he did at least once a day, he took out the worn picture of his two-year-old son, Edgar. The boy was round-faced with curly blond hair. He had more of Edith's features than his own, the bushy eyebrows the only trait that seemed to come from his father. Edgar, his prince. At one point in the war, Beyer had fought for the Fatherland, believed in the need for a bigger Germany. But now he could see how the army was used. Hitler had abandoned them. Even Rommel had been ordered out of Africa so he would not be associated with their defeat. Now Beyer fought only for family, his wife and son. They were what motivated him, gave him the will to fight on.

The planes had been gone little more than twenty minutes when Beyer heard the high-pitched drone of a plane diving. He knew before his brain could even register to run. *British fighters.* He cursed himself for not continuing to watch. The planes came out of the west, diving out of the clouds so the sun blotted out their approach.

Three Hurricanes, just above tree level. Beyer yelled to take cover and ran toward the nearest bunker. He seemed to be moving in slow motion, the sand sucking at his boots. He could hear the 20-millimeter flak gun at the edge of the field firing volley after volley. *Get the sons-of-bitches.* The roar of the

Hurricanes' engines grew louder: from each wing bullets kicked up sand to his left, screeching as they drew deadly lines in the sand, then a hot gust of wind buffeted him as the planes passed. Beyer dove for the bunker like a swimmer starting a race, landing in a tangle of five other men. He took a quick inventory. All were men from Baade's detail.

"Where is Sergeant Baade?" Beyer yelled.

A fair-complected private, still a boy, cowered next to Beyer. The boy's hands trembled.

"Sergeant Baade?" Beyer shook the boy. He looked up, his eyes irrational, ready to bolt. Beyer screamed, "Baade, where is he?"

"Trading for eggs with one of the Africans," the boy said.

Two Africans had arrived by donkey earlier in the morning trying to barter for pieces of his men's uniforms until Beyer had run them off. It was a court-martial offense to sell their uniforms, and more importantly, headquarters had warned that some of the Africans might be spying for the British.

Beyer heard the Hurricanes' engines laboring as they climbed to make another strafing run. Fat Sergeant Baade, always hungry. Baade had been a cook in Hanau before the war and suffered more than most on the low rations. To risk dying for a couple of eggs. Beyer shook his head. If Baade were very lucky, he may have been able to find cover in the mosque.

The Hurricanes began their descent: a piercing scream, then the rattle of machine guns, echoed by the pounding of the flak gun. This time the planes were on target. A terrible explosion shook the ground as heat scorched Beyer's back. *Fuel dump.* A few seconds later, smaller explosions erupted, touched off by the fire. Beyer listened for the ascent of the Hurricanes, dreading their next run. But just as suddenly as the planes had appeared, their engines faded away—onto another target.

The men hunkered close to the ground for several more minutes, not wanting to take a chance on another surprise attack. Finally, Beyer peered above the bunker. He found everything obscured by thick black smoke, and from within it, bright flames leaped thirty meters into the sky from the burning fuel depot. The fire was so intense it was impossible to look directly at it for more than a few seconds. Two of the Stukas they had worked on for a week were on fire, their skins burned off to the frames.

The smoke made breathing difficult, so Beyer took his handkerchief, dabbed it with water from his canteen, and tied it around his face. He hurried to the other bunkers, taking a quick accounting of his men.

A strange, almost human noise was coming from the airstrip, so Beyer shielded his eyes and edged out toward the fuel depot. Ten meters out he heard what sounded like crying, human at first, then not. After a few more steps, Beyer made out what appeared to be two charred gray blankets and a dark form bending over them. A huge dog? A few steps closer and it all came into focus. The Africans' donkey stood over one of its masters braying loudly, its fur still smoldering from the fuel explosion. The donkey nudged a foot, found no movement, then bawled more loudly. Evidently, Baade and the Africans had been caught out in the open and had no chance to make it to the mosque. Instead, they had run toward the bunkers and been chewed up by the Hurricanes' machine guns. Baade lay facedown, his arm reaching unnaturally behind him for something. His lost eggs.

A wild rage built in Beyer's throat, choking him. Was this what the war was about? If he thought the Hurricane pilots could have heard him, he would have screamed: "You have killed a decent man, a father of two young boys, a good husband. He was a wonderful cook who planned to open a *gasthaus* adjoining his father's butcher shop when the war was over. His wife, Ute, will not understand why this needed to happen. His family needed him more than this war." But no words came. The wind and heat of the fire dried Beyer's tears. He could do nothing more for Sergeant Baade. He edged away from the heat of the fire. They would need to remove the bodies and donkey as soon as the heat subsided in case any of the planes needed to make an emergency landing.

Beyer returned to his bunker and told the men to form a burial detail for the three dead men, while he checked the remaining damage. He would say a prayer for them when he finished. To Beyer's surprise, the strafing had missed a cache of bombs and machine-gun ammunition in a camouflaged bunker. A small bit of luck. He stepped down into the pit and began taking inventory. Five to six days at the maximum.

"What then?" he asked out loud. "On to Cairo," he

shouted, then began to laugh. "On to London, on to New York." He laughed hysterically. It helped drain the rage he felt on seeing Baade. He laughed so hard that he did not hear the captain calling his name until he was almost in the bunker.

Captain Hinz stood at the top of the bunker looking quizzically at Beyer. "Are you all right?"

Hinz was the same age as Beyer, thirty-two, but the war had aged his face prematurely, deep crow's-feet etched around the eyes, his blond hair streaked gray at the sides. He had been a pilot before he injured his arm, and seemed lost now that he'd been placed in command of the ground unit.

Beyer came to attention, ashamed to have lost his bearing. "Sorry, sir. Sergeant Baade is dead."

"I know," Captain Hinz said sadly. Then after a long silence his command voice returned. "Gather your men and any of the ammunition you can carry, and be ready to move out in a half hour. I just received a radio call that we are being pulled back to an airstrip near Tunis."

A brief reprieve, thought Beyer. Perhaps he wouldn't die today. Still, it was hard to think of blowing up planes they had been working on for days.

Beyer asked, "And the remaining bombs?"

"Anything you cannot carry, destroy. Make sure you burn any documents."

Beyer saluted, climbed out of the bunker, and went to oversee the burial. His men had already dug shallow graves, then covered them with rocks to keep the animals away. A hastily constructed wooden cross stood at the front of Baade's grave with his Pith helmet on top. Beyer's men stood at attention, many of them crying.

Beyer knelt to pray. "Sergeant Baade was a good man, brave, our comrade. We all knew and loved him. God protect his soul and bring peace to his loved ones. Amen." He stood and put his helmet back on. "We are pulling out. Destroy everything."

The men gave each other curious glances, but said nothing. They shuffled away and began carrying out Beyer's orders.

A half hour later the nineteen men left in Beyer's command sat in the bed of a half-track as it left the airstrip of Mejez el Bab. When they were several kilometers away, the bombs began to explode, the ash, smoke, and sand blackening the sky.

Two weeks later Beyer lay asleep in a foxhole outside an airfield near Tunis. They were just far enough from the Mediterranean that the sea breezes did not reach them during the day, yet they suffered desert cold at night. Beyer slept uneasily, dreaming of Hamburg again, his city of a thousand bridges, Germany's Venice. In his dream he was trying to find the bridge into Altoona, the city contiguous to Hamburg, that for centuries had served as sanctuary and safe haven for political refugees. Now that he was rationed to a quarter of a canteen a day, his dreams were always about water. This worried him because of what the fortune-teller had said to him in January.

Beyer had not wanted to go, but Edith had talked him into seeing the old gypsy woman while he was on leave. Edith claimed that the woman had brought one of her friend's husbands good luck. So they had gone to an old apartment down by the harbor that was full of cats and the smell of rancid cooked cabbage. The old woman wore a purple scarf on her head and many bangles around her wrists, and had insisted on being paid before she looked at the crystal ball. After much hand waving over the ball, the gypsy gasped and said, "Do not go across the water. There is extreme danger for you there." Edith had run out terrified. Beyer thought it merely a scam to obtain more money to avoid the curse. But now he was not as sure, and his nightly dreams about water worried him.

Tonight's dream had rain and loud thundering; it became so loud that he awoke. He realized that it was not thunder at all, but artillery. The western sky erupted with red and yellow flashes, and in the distance he could hear the crackle of small arms fire. He pulled his overcoat tighter against the desert cold, but realized he would never fall back to sleep. It was already near dawn, and the air was mixed with the smells of charcoal fires and jasmine. Some of his men were boiling water for ersatz coffee, the only ration they had left. They had not eaten in two days. Beyer pulled himself wearily from his foxhole, his body stiff from lying on the ground.

He watched the artillery fire and hoped the Americans would push through and get it over with. Better to die in battle than to starve to death. Any fight would be quick, since they were out of ammunition and the planes that could fly had been sent back to Sicily. What remained around the airfield was a junkyard: JU52 transports with their corrugated bodies twisted by bombs, Focke-Wulfs and Messerschmitts reduced to skeletons by strafing and fire. For a week now there had been rumors of surrender, false hopes that ships were being sent to rescue them. Lies. Beyer was not afraid to die. What angered him was to die for more lies. Just tell them the truth! We have abandoned you, and we no longer care. We have other battles that we are fighting now.

Then at midmorning word spread among the clusters of men that an important formation would be held at noon. There was talk of surrender. The men debated whether it was better to be taken by the Americans or the Brits. Wild rumors spread about slave labor camps run by the British, where you were forced to sleep in damp warehouses and men died by the hundreds of pneumonia. Beyer recognized it as propaganda that had been put on the radio earlier in the war to keep men from surrendering. If there was a choice, Beyer preferred the Americans. His brother, Karl, lived in America and worked on an air force base in Mississippi. Often Beyer received letters about how good the life was, how his brother had a great job and had married an American woman. Yes, if he had any chance, he preferred to be captured by the Americans. But Beyer stayed out of the conversations and did not mention his brother. He had seen enough false alarms about surrendering to know this could be nothing as well.

But, as rumored, at exactly noon the wing commander called a formation of all the aircrews that were left. The colonel, an old man wearing his white Luftwaffe dress uniform, stood on a maintenance ladder in the boiling sun and read the following message from the Führer:

I express my thanks and deepest appreciation to you and your heroically fighting troops, who in the true comradeship in arms with your Italian comrades defended every foot of African soil. It was with admiration that the entire German people watched with me the heroic battle of your soldiers in Tunisia. It has been of the greatest significance to the overall success of the war. The final action and conduct of your troops will be an example for the entire armed forces of the Greater German Reich and serve as an especially glorious page in the history of German warfare. Signed Adolf Hitler.

The colonel tucked the message away in his breast pocket, then saluted. A rousing *"Heil Hitler"* came from the assembled men.

"We will march in ranks back to Mejez el Bab," the colonel instructed. "There, I have been told, we will become prisoners of the British."

The men gathered up all their belongings and formed into ranks. Beyer gave the order for left face, and they began their march. They became a long gray river—AAA crews, paratroopers, and members of the Hermann Göring Division—coming out of every ditch and ravine and cave along the road, until there were more than five thousand men on the road. The march was slow, because the road south had been turned into a graveyard of twisted tanks and half-tracks. The fortune-teller had been wrong, thought Beyer. He was out of the war now. Safe. He would be fine, as long as he remembered who he was. "You are a German, a soldier." He repeated it several times to himself. He made sure he told every one of his men: "You are a German, a soldier. Do not forget who you are."

2

Stranger in a Strange Land

Somewhere in the Mid-Atlantic
June 1943

CORPORAL JOHANNES KUNZE, ALONG WITH FIFTY OTHER German POWs, lay in his hammock in the hold of the converted Liberty ship steaming toward America. After their capture in Tunisia, Kunze and the others had been shipped to Bournemouth, England, but their stay had been short-lived. On their first night in the camp, a torch-bearing mob of local Brits, many of whom had lost loved ones in the fighting, showed up with clubs and bricks intent on evening the score. Baton-wielding MPs were finally forced to crack a few skulls before the mob decided to retreat to the local pub. Several POWs suffered minor injuries from flying bricks and rocks, and the local authorities quickly decided they couldn't handle the situation. A week later officials from the Red Cross and an anxious-looking British colonel told the camp they were being moved. "America will be quite different," the British colonel assured the POWs as they were loaded back onto the boats. "Those Yanks are a different lot."

The colonel was not telling Kunze anything he hadn't already thought about. America was going to be where Kunze would change his life forever. He thought about it constantly and learned to build it like a wall to shut out the long ocean voyage. First he would persuade the army to transfer him to a camp in California. Kunze was floating in this fantasy about his new life, when the ship suddenly listed hard to the right. Lights flickered, then blacked out.

"Where is the auxiliary generator?" someone shouted.

Again they were tossed back and forth in their bunks. Kunze could hear several men retching violently in the corner. A man near him was reciting the Lord's prayer.

"U-Boat!" someone speculated.

The word brought the coppery taste of dread to Kunze's mouth. On the way to North Africa from Naples, he had seen two troop ships hit by torpedoes. It was a horrible death: trapped belowdeck, drowning in the dark, then your body floating to the surface, where it became food for gulls and sharks. A man deserved a better end, thought Kunze. Still, they waited, listening for an explosion, for the sound of gushing water. The air was thick with the smells of diesel fumes and bile. Without a destroyer escort, the Liberty ships were easy targets. There was simply no justice in being killed by your own countrymen, thought Kunze.

Five minutes later the big generator whined back to life, and the lights returned. Rough seas. A wave of relief drifted from bunk to bunk. They murmured *"insa' Allah,"* the Moslem plea for divine intercession that so many had used during the fighting in the desert. "The sharks will have to look elsewhere tonight," someone yelled—more gallows humor. "Our comrades must be looking for other American ships."

Sergeant Major Richter, a tall, wiry man with a pockmarked face and thinning black hair, rose from his hammock, stood at attention, and began to sing the German national anthem.

"Deutschland, Deutschland uber alles."

The men rolled out of their bunks, came to attention, and sang proudly. Reluctantly, Kunze stood and sang without enthusiasm.

"From the Oder in the East to the Rhine in the West. Germany, Germany everywhere."

With each verse, the singing puffed them up with beer-hall bravado. After the fifth verse Sergeant Major Richter raised his hand to speak.

"To our fallen comrades in Africa. *Heil Hitler!*"

"Heil Hitler" came the shouted response, arms raised in salute.

Richter's voice quivered with reverence. "To our great leader, Field Marshal Erwin Rommel."

"Heil Hitler."

"To the Hermann Göring Division. . . ."

Kunze lay back down on his hammock. He felt all of his forty years tonight. His gums bled from the poor fit of his false teeth. All those years when they'd not had any meat and survived on potatoes were taking their toll. Just this morning he had noticed how his coarse brown hair was speckled with gray and receding at the temples. He was too old for this war. The Nazis had tried to make him an infantryman, put him in the famed Hermann Göring Division, and told him he was an Aryan superman. How laughable. He was a machinist. Always would be. Just look at him. Short and squat, with a broad face and a lantern jaw. Only his wife, Erna, who saw him with her heart, noticed anything special in him. "You have beautiful blue eyes," she had cooed at him when they were teenagers.

When the singing stopped, Sergeant Koch, a baby-faced blond who had been a leader in the Hitler Youth in Frankfurt, leaned down from his bunk. "Kunze, you did not sing much. Are you sick?"

Kunze puffed the idea away. "I am done with Germany," he said. "When the war is over," he held up a finger for emphasis, "I will bring my family to America. Start over."

Koch squinted, then shook his head. "Those are very dangerous thoughts to have, my friend. Back home people go up in smoke for even thinking such things."

How well Kunze knew. Back home in Leipzig his uncle Leo, the communist labor leader, had been taken away in the middle of the night, shipped to Dachau, then never heard from again. "Brown Shirt thugs," the neighbors had told him. "Don't ask any more questions or you will be next." Germany's lunacy was past them now. Whether Sergeant Koch realized it or not, they had new masters. Soon the

Americans would control every facet of their lives, and Kunze was ready.

"We are not in Germany anymore, my friend," said Kunze. "You'd better get used to it."

The young sergeant wagged his finger. "One defeat does not mean the war is over. When we reach America, you will see, Kunze. Our planes have been bombing their cities for months." With that Koch rolled back up into his bunk.

Brainwashed! thought Kunze. Sergeant Koch and so many like him were the problem. Couldn't they see what the crazy little corporal was doing? Thousands had died in North Africa, and for what? To surrender a piece of sand, to save face for the Italians. And their great leader, Rommel. *Mein Gott.* He had left them before the fighting was even over. How many died of thirst in the desert? What kind of leaders expected them to fight even when they were out of ammunition? Was it any wonder that Germany was being reduced to rubble on a daily basis. They sang of the homeland, but what was the use if you had no home to return to after the war?

No, Kunze had figured out the answer. When they arrived in the United States, the Americans would need help: a bit of information about his old unit, who the Nazi leaders were in the group. In turn, he was certain the Americans would reward him.

Kunze closed his eyes again and returned to his dream of life in America. Once the war was over, he would build a home by the Pacific Ocean. Then he would start his own tool and die works. He saw himself sitting on the beach with Erna, the three children playing in the waves, the ocean shimmering in the evening light like a thousand gold coins. Paradise. He savored the scene, holding the image of his new life in his mind until it drew him toward a warm sleep.

A week later Kunze and a thousand other members of the Afrika Korps landed in Norfolk, Virginia. It was a relief just to see the sky again, even though Norfolk's thick, brackish air was hot as an oven. From the deck of the ship, Kunze got a quick glimpse of palm-lined streets and beautiful colonial homes near Norfolk's harbor. Cars and trucks sped down a nearby highway. This was not a nation being bombed on a daily basis, thought Kunze. Germany had taken on a formidable foe that would not be turned back. It was just a matter of time.

Kunze made it a point to fall in line behind Sergeant Koch as they walked down the gangplank toward the waiting rail cars.

"Our bombers must have missed, eh, Koch?"

Koch looked around and quickly pronounced, "They have simply repaired the damage. We will destroy it again."

There was simply no hope for Nazis like Koch. He would go to his grave believing the Third Reich was on the verge of taking over the world. The Americans would surely want to know about men like Koch, so they could keep them from starting trouble.

The train ride to their new home was slow and

uncomfortable. Fifty men were assigned to every car. Two MPs were in each compartment, one at the front and one at the rear. There was no room to stretch out and sleep, so men dozed as best they could while leaning against one another. One of the guards offered the man in front of Kunze an American newspaper, but Sergeant Major Richter interceded and tore it up, saying that he would not have his men's minds polluted with propaganda. As a result, the only real entertainment was to stare out the top six inches of the train window that had not been blacked out.

Two days into the trip—Tennessee—Kunze's legs could not take any more of the standing. He resolved to try and sleep, even though it was nearly impossible because of the rough track and constant jostling of the other men to peer out the windows. Kunze was almost asleep when a loud wolf's whistle woke him.

"Look," Sergeant Major Richter said boastfully. "Women for hire."

All the men in the compartment quickly pushed to Kunze's side of the train. He had no choice but to stand. There in a cornfield was a big-boned brunet woman and two teenaged girls wearing identical flowered dresses. All the women had their hair tied back with red bandannas. A man stood behind a mule and plow, eating something they had obviously brought him.

"How much do you think they go for?" asked Sergeant Koch.

"Cheap," Richter answered. "They are worse than the Italian women in Tunis.

The men laughed uproariously.

"All their women are whores," Richter pronounced.

In Germany a decent man would be thrown out of a *gasthaus* for talking about the local women this way. It was a sign of how far his homeland had degenerated that a man like Richter was in charge of the battalion. And Richter talked about being the master race? Germany was no longer the kind of country where Kunze wanted his wife and daughter to live.

The train lumbered on, passing long fields of tobacco and alfalfa. Richter smiled and addressed the group. "Many fields, rich soil, many automobiles, all this will be our colony someday."

The men mumbled agreement, but Kunze knew this was only dreaming. There would be no taking this land from the Americans. There was simply too much of everything. Too much land, too many people with resolve for Germany to ever overcome. Kunze had already seen how tenacious the Americans had been in North Africa.

The next day word spread down the cars that they were nearing their destination of Tonkawa, Oklahoma. The land had changed from rolling hills to flat open space, where the crop was wheat and the people seemed to have totally disappeared. The people lived so many kilometers apart that a half hour would go by and they would only see a small white farmhouse or a patch of oil derricks the entire time. To Kunze, the sky seemed as blue and vast as any he'd seen in the desert. On the train journey several of the men had whispered of escaping, but this land confirmed the futility of that talk. They were thousands of kilometers away from the nearest ocean, with no friendly civilians to give aid and assistance and, most important, a language that gave them away immediately as the enemy. No, he had certainly made the right choice. Let the others escape if they wanted.

The train ran parallel to a highway as they neared the town of Tonkawa, the blacktop shimmering heat vapors. Soon the engineer began blowing his whistle to announce their arrival. As they inched along the outskirts of Tonkawa with its wide streets and clapboard houses, it seemed to Kunze that the entire town had turned out to meet them. Young boys were perched in trees acting as lookouts for the train; farmers dressed in overalls and straw hats stood in wagon beds, many with binoculars, making sure they missed nothing; entire families, some still eating their picnic lunches, leaped to their feet to get a view of the Krauts, children clambering to mount their father's shoulders so they, too, might have this first glimpse of the enemy.

The train moved to farmland north of town, where American MPs materialized in force. Kunze estimated at least a company. Their black helmets and brass belt buckles sparkled in the hot August sun. They seemed to be taking silly precautions. Every twenty kilometers along the line of march from the train to the compound, MPs stood cradling shotguns, many of them nervously fingering the safeties off. Fifty-caliber machine guns were positioned on the compound roofs, aimed at their line of march. The squat octagonal guard towers located at every corner of the compound were manned, and their machine guns traced every step the prisoners made.

The men joked about how dangerous they were, then formed in ranks to march to the compound. Secretly Kunze liked what he saw. The Americans were in charge, there would be no bullying by the Nazi thugs. This display of force was meant to show that.

Their new home wasn't that much different from barracks Kunze had suffered during his basic training. Long, single-story wooden buildings covered in tar paper were arranged into three compounds, ten barracks to a compound. Each compound had its own clinic, administration office, and outside latrine. And from what Kunze could see as they marched into camp, there was a large soccer field and hospital. The entire camp was laid out in a huge field with no houses around for several kilometers. None of it mattered much, because Kunze did not plan to stay here long.

Kunze had mug shots taken, was fingerprinted, then issued black denim fatigues with the large letters "POW" stenciled on the back. He was glad to shed his Afrika Korps tunic. Another life, like shedding damaged skin. As he passed by the final table, the clerk assigned him to Compound I, Company Four, commanded by First Sergeant Walter Beyer.

At his barracks Kunze unpacked his personal belonging into the footlocker he'd been provided. He was just in the process of making up his cot, when an MP sergeant and tall officer appeared in the door of his barracks.

"Kunze?" the officer inquired.

The corporal held up his hand.

"Arbeit." The American sergeant held up a broom and motioned for Kunze to follow them.

Kunze shrugged and smiled at his comrades. Once he provided the Americans information, they wouldn't treat him this way. He would be given the easy jobs.

Before he reached the door, First Sergeant Beyer stopped him. From what Kunze had seen of Beyer on the train, he knew the man was grimly serious, and not someone to be trifled with. First Sergeant Beyer moved close and whispered, "Corporal, be very careful. The Americans will try to turn you against your country. Always remember that you are a German, a soldier."

Kunze smiled nervously. There was no way Beyer could read his mind. Besides, he hadn't even approached the Americans yet. "Don't worry about me, First Sergeant."

With that Kunze left the barracks and followed the Americans to a small building at the edge of the compound that read "Administration." The sergeant gave Kunze the broom and motioned for him to go in and begin sweeping.

As the door closed behind him, Kunze took a step and found himself tangled in a mass of cobwebs. He slapped furiously at his face, terrified of a spider. There seemed to be a presence looming in the corner. Kunze raised his broom, ready to club it. It took several minutes for his eyes to adjust to the dim light before he could make out that the room was really empty except for a pile of mattresses in the corner. All the windows were closed, and it was suffocatingly hot. Why are they doing this to me? thought Kunze. Could it be a tactic to break me down? Just do as you are told, he reassured himself, it will all work out. Kunze went to the window and began to open it, when he heard the door open and close behind him. He jumped at the unexpected appearance of a man in a dark brown suit in front of the door.

"I hope the work is not too hard," the man said in perfect German.

Though the man was in civilian clothing, his bearing was military, probably an officer. From what Kunze could see of him in the half-light, he had thinning blond hair and wore wire-rim glasses.

"It is awfully hot in here," Kunze said.

The man removed his hat and stepped into view. His teeth were crooked and yellowed. He gave the appearance of not being healthy, as if he might have jaundice. "We won't be long." The man offered Kunze a cigarette and lit it. The tobacco tasted delicious. Kunze smoked hungrily, then began coughing.

"I'm Major Dietrich, in charge of security for this area. It's my understanding that you might be willing to help us."

He must think quickly. This might be his only chance to convince the Americans he was valuable. Yet, he must not sell himself short. Make them give you firm commitments, before you agree to anything.

"Perhaps," Kunze said, trying to sound cagey. "But if I do, you must make sure I'm transferred out of here."

He watched Major Dietrich nod, as if that were no problem.

Emboldened, Kunze added, "And I want to be sent to California. If you can't send me to California, I'm not interested."

Dietrich studied him a long minute. He watched Kunze finish the cigarette, then offered him another and stuck the remaining pack into Kunze's pocket.

"I think we could work something out." Dietrich moistened his lips. "Provided you give us valuable information. We want to know about any escape attempts, any Nazis who might be planning trouble for us. Also any military information you hear. Even if it is old. It still might be valuable. Do you understand?"

Kunze nodded. His uniform was drenched with sweat. The cigarette and heat were making him lightheaded, but he could not pass out in front of this major and show his weakness. The American might think Kunze lacked the courage to fulfill his end of the bargain.

"Anytime you have information, you can give it to any officer here. They'll make sure I receive it. Any questions?"

He had many. Should he write out notes? How would he manage to be alone with an American officer without the other men knowing? Would there be a way to signal if he were in any danger? The questions raced around his brain. The room was hotter than the worst days he could remember in the desert. You must not let this officer think you don't know what you're doing. He would figure these details out himself.

Dietrich extended his hand, his grip bone crushingly strong for such a thin man. He said, "You've done the right thing."

3

Traitor in Our Midst

POW Camp, Tonkawa, Oklahoma
September 1943

FIRST SERGEANT BEYER SAT ON HIS FOOTLOCKER WRITING a letter to his wife. He had sent Edith two letters per week since he arrived in August, yet by late September he still had not received a reply. The Swiss representative from the Red Cross said it might take six months for his letters to even reach Germany. The silence from home played horrible tricks on his mind. Were Edith and the boy all right? Had they given him up for dead? Did anyone care whether he was still alive?

He stopped a moment and watched Frans Beidle paint another scene on the rough wooden barracks walls. Beidle had managed to brighten the barracks with several Bavarian mountain scenes, and now the Berlin city crest. A large bear stood atop a shield that Beidle was striping red and white. Beyer wished he could find a hobby to divert his thinking about the danger back home. His nerves were shattered, his comrades told him often.

He had the same dream at least once a week. In his

nightmare, Edith and Edgar were at the Hamburg open-air market near the train station when a bombing raid began. The antiaircraft guns blotched the sky with white clouds of shrapnel, but the hundreds of American B-29s droned above the city anyway, unleashing their screaming bundles of destruction. The market quickly broke into pandemonium: carts overturned, people fell, children screamed. The crowd moved like a rough wave pushing people out and toward the surrounding buildings. As Edith ran for shelter, somehow she lost hold of Edgar's hand and he was swallowed by the chaos of the market. Edith tried to turn and grab the boy, but the crowd kept pushing her farther away. Then suddenly Beyer appeared in his dream. He fought back through the crowd searching for Edgar among the fleeing women and children. Beyer asked everyone he met about the boy, but they seemed not to see or hear him. All around him bombs crumbled huge buildings to rubble. The air was choked with gray dust. Then he saw a small hand under a pile of bricks and girders. It grasped the air, at once beckoning and reaching for help. Closer, there was no mistaking the voice. Edgar, his little prince, calling: "Papa, help me!" And when Beyer tried to move the bricks to uncover the boy, Edgar kept sinking farther and farther beneath the rubble. Beyer would wake, soaked with sweat and screaming the boy's name.

Beyer knew the source of the dream. A month earlier Sergeant Seidel had smuggled a copy of the *Tulsa Tribune* from his job at the camp administration building. On the front page were pictures of

Hamburg and Cologne reduced to smoking piles of rubble under the headline: NAZI CITIES PAY THE PRICE. It was impossible to tell from the pictures how much damage the cities had sustained. Beyer resolved never to look at the paper again, but found himself sneaking glimpses, finding the imagined damage more torturous than what he could discern from the pictures.

Finally, he put pen to paper, resolving not to let Edith know his fears.

My Dear Dear wife Edith & Edgar:
    Today I was thinking of the times we hiked in the Black Forest. That seems a lifetime ago. Then later I remembered when we were first married. I would rush down to find you in your kimono and think how beautiful you looked. I was so worried about your pregnancy. I was reading a book about love last week and was inspired to write about it myself. Now I realize that love can only come during marriage.

Beyer heard the low voice of the "priest," Victor Zorzi, talking to Beidle. Zorzi was not really a priest, having studied only six semesters for the priesthood, but the men thought of him as one of their religious leaders. He was a ghostly looking figure, tall, with a cadaverous face and thinning red hair. His watery blue eyes seemed faded with sadness. He spoke a moment longer to Beidle, then approached Beyer.

"First Sergeant, any news from your family?"

Beyer shook his head "no." Zorzi's family lived in Altoona, the city connected to Hamburg.

"Priest, do you have any news?"

Zorzi sighed deeply, shut his eyes. "My aunt was killed last week. The Red Cross brought the news today. There seems no place left that is safe."

There was a hopeless inevitability in Zorzi's statement, as if sooner or later all German civilians would be killed by the Allied bombing.

"I will ask my wife to check on your mother and father." Beyer drew on his command voice, formal, brusque. He did not want to linger on the thought.

"I will pray for all our families," Zorzi said, sweeping his hand to include the entire camp. His priestly visit paid, Zorzi wandered to the end of the barracks to warm himself by the coal stove.

Beyer began again, determined to put this letter in the mail. He tried not to think of Zorzi's bad news, but he found it creeping into his letter.

My little rascal, I am suffering because I don't know what is happening, whether fate has taken my wife and child from me. But I am too much of a coward not to think that you are okay. Please give the boy my love. A thousand kisses, Edgar.

It was not what he wanted, too self-pitying. Edith and the boy were in harm's way now, not him. He sealed the pale green POW stationery along the prescribed lines and tucked it into his pocket for the mail. He would make his daily inspection and try not to think of home for a while.

The walk helped clear his head. The afternoon was warm and clear with just the first hint of fall's decay in the air. Beyer strode up the wooden sidewalk toward the company mess hall: a long, single-storied tar-paper building that the men had beautified by wiring off flower beds around the entrance. After the hunger in Tunisia, Beyer savored his daily tour of the mess hall with its assurance that there would always be plenty to eat.

As Beyer crossed the street to the mess hall's back entrance, he passed a gray-haired American lieutenant who worked in the infirmary.

"Heil Hitler," Beyer said, giving the stiff-armed salute.

The lieutenant turned on his heels and hurried back to Beyer. "Hold it right there, buddy."

Beyer stopped, came to attention. What was the problem? He'd shown the proper respect. The old lieutenant eyeballed Beyer.

"No more of that Nazi crap, understand? *Verstehan sie?"* The lieutenant's face flushed red as he tried to correct Beyer, his double chin wiggling as he lectured. "I am an American officer. *Amerikan officer! Nicht, Deutschland.* We're in America now."

The lieutenant paused a moment, seeming to search for the right scrap of German. *"Kein mar . . .* Oh, hells bells," he said, stammering for another word. "I don't ever want to catch you doing that again." He gave the stiff armed salute, then yanked his arm down. *"Kein, Heil Hitler. Verstehan sie?"*

They could not stop him from being a German soldier. The sergeant major had already had an argument about this with the camp commandant. Being a soldier was the one thread that held the men together;

it made this separation bearable. Beyer looked stoically ahead.

When it became apparent that he wasn't going to react, the old lieutenant stomped off muttering, "Goddamn Krauts."

Beyer smiled. Americans! Petulant, undisciplined, overfed—the old lieutenant never could have been a German officer.

A crew of ten men were in the kitchen preparing supper when Beyer entered the mess hall. They seemed in good cheer as they talked to one another and listened to big-band music on a radio the Americans had loaned them. They had worked out an assembly line where a couple of men cut whole chickens into parts, another three dipped the parts into batter, and the others lay the pieces in large frying pans for the new dish the Americans had shown them. The smell of fried chicken and potatoes wafted through the mess hall. It made Beyer proud to see his men work like this, the same precision he saw and expected on his flight line. He was almost ready to leave, when he noticed that one man was not working.

Johannes Kunze. The old corporal sat on an overturned bucket talking, but not helping. Beyer had received reports about Kunze's back talk, his refusal to follow orders, and his general attitude that he was better than the other men; Beyer intended to put a quick stop to it.

He crept up silently behind Kunze. Slowly, the other men noticed the first sergeant and stopped their conversations. Someone must have motioned with his eyes to Kunze, because he turned and grinned sheepishly.

"Why are you not helping the other men? This is your detail."

Kunze shrugged. "I am not as young as these other men."

When Beyer shook his head in disgust, Kunze's tone turned a bit insolent. "We are not in Germany anymore. This is no longer the place for orders. I've worked plenty."

Without another word, Beyer drew his leg back and kicked the bucket out from under Kunze. He lay sprawled on the floor for a few seconds, then drew himself out of range of the first sergeant's boot. The other men roared. The man knew better. He was not a boy. No one in the German Army should act this way. Yes, they were not in Germany any longer and lucky for Kunze. For Beyer would have had him court-martialed.

"Every man works here. You are no better than anyone else."

Beyer stood with his hands on his hips, glaring at Kunze, daring him to make a response. But Kunze merely pulled himself to his feet, his face sullen and angry. He put on his apron, found a meat cleaver, and began hacking at the chickens.

This was why they had lost in the desert, thought Beyer. Too many men like Kunze. Too many draftees who had no love for their country. As the battle for North Africa dragged on, the ranks of the Afrika

Korps had been filled with Poles and Czechs, men who could barely speak German, and old conscripts like Kunze, all of whom did not want to be there. And if the truth were ever known, probably didn't care if Germany won or lost. Beyer's time in the camp had made him realize the truth about the proud German Army. He could not change what happened in Africa, but he could surely control the men of his company and they would be good German soldiers whether they wanted to be or not.

Three days later Beyer was playing soccer, passing a shot off to his forward, when he saw Achilles Rehberger signaling him to come to the sideline. He watched a forward angle in a quick shot, which the goalie dove for and stopped. Beyer trotted to the sideline and asked one of his teammates to replace him.

"What is it?" Beyer used his shirt to towel his forehead. Though the evenings were chilly, October still brought warm days. Indian summer, the Americans called it.

Rehberger, a broad-faced blond with shy blue eyes, seemed hesitant to say anything. "Please not here, First Sergeant. There is something urgent that I must show you." He motioned with his eyes back toward the barracks.

"Just walk with me. We will draw suspicion if we return to the barracks." Beyer bent down and massaged his calf, as if he had a charley horse. He limped away from the sidelines shaking his leg.

"What has happened?" Beyer asked.

Rehberger took out his pouch of tobacco and papers, then seemed to inadvertently drop a cigarette paper. Beyer picked up the tissue-like paper and read in bold German cursive: "Have information."

"Where did you find this?"

Rehberger rolled a cigarette and lit it. "Heisig. He took it from a desk in the infirmary."

"Does he know who?"

Rehberger shook his head. "He found it right after our company had gone through for typhoid shots. It is definitely one of the men, that's all he knows."

The thought sickened Beyer. Traitor, turncoat, Judas, a spy in their midst. Worse, a member of his company. Ready to sell out his comrades, his country, for some false hope the Americans might promise. There could be nothing lower. They must catch the vermin quickly before he has a chance to do any damage.

"You have done well, Achilles." Beyer patted him on the back. "Have Heisig keep his eyes open."

"First Sergeant, how will you catch him?"

The traitor had not been smart. He had written the note in his own hand, and there was a unique curve to the way he made his *z*. Every man in the company wrote home at least once a week. Some like Beyer wrote several times a week. Unless the traitor was disguising his handwriting, they would soon a have an example to compare with the note.

"From now on I will act as a censor for the mail. Have Sergeant Seidel bring me the mail."

Beyer turned back to the field. The thought sickened him: the man ate and slept with them every day, pretending to be their comrade. He watched a player kick a shot hard and high into the goal. Be patient, he told himself, a rat will come out for food, no matter what the risk.

4

The Ticket to California

POW Camp, Tonkawa, Oklahoma
Early November, 1943

THE FIRST HARD FROST HAD COME DURING THE NIGHT, gnarling the grass around the barracks, coating the sidewalks and roofs with a shiny film of ice. The men of Company Four stood at attention, their collective breaths rising like smoke from a fast-moving train. Kunze had positioned himself at the far end of the second platoon, out of First Sergeant Beyer's line of sight, and quietly waited for sick call. He stared at the morning sky, bruised purple with a flush of crimson on the lip of the horizon and thought about a California sunrise. Kunze knew it would be better somehow: brighter, warmer, with a hint of the ocean in it.

The northwest wind gusted hard, and Kunze felt a chill coming. Good. The sicker he looked the better. During the night he had sneaked out of bed and put on two pairs of long underwear, his fatigues, his overcoat, and covered himself with two extra blankets. He'd even eaten a little soap to upset his stomach. He would claim it was the flu, maybe the first signs of pneumonia. Plenty of the guards had already been sick this week, and even Beyer, with his constant suspicions, would not risk having someone die in his charge.

There had been no choice but to fake illness again so he could go to the infirmary where the reception sergeant knew to send him to his handler, Major Dietrich. For a week he'd been attempting to pass information to the officer in charge of the mess hall, to no avail. One of his comrades always seemed to be shadowing him. He knew he'd been drawing too much attention to himself by faking illness so often, but he was so close to the Americans letting him go. Dietrich had wanted important information: "No more notes about North Africa," he warned. "That's worthless to us now. We need to know about targets in Germany, potential problems in the camp. You come up with some more of that, and I'll guarantee you a transfer. California, just like you requested."

Now Kunze had information.

"Sick call," First Sergeant Beyer finally announced.

Private Ingall in the first platoon and Kunze stepped forward.

It felt as if every eye in the company was on him. *They know.* No, not possible, he told himself. He had scribbled the information while he sat in the latrine, then carried the note on his person ever since. And as far as he could remember, there had been no signs of animosity. Achilles Rehberger continued to teach him to play chess. No one seemed concerned at his effort to learn English. All senseless worry. Keep your nerve, this will be the last time you'll have to go through this charade.

The first sergeant huddled with Ingall, putting his hand on his shoulder, inquiring about his condition in a fatherly tone. Then he regained his military bearing, did a sharp left face, and marched to Kunze.

Slowly, Beyer looked him over as he would for inspection, not saying anything for a long time. Kunze tried to make his body sag, as if under the weight of some great fatigue. The nippy air made him shiver again. He could feel the sweat on his forehead.

Finally, Beyer addressed him. "What's the problem, Corporal. Too sick to cook?"

Kunze smiled sadly, then coughed. "I believe the flu, First Sergeant. It feels as if it might be moving to my chest." He looked at the ground, trying to avoid Beyer's stare. A million times Kunze reproached himself for angering Beyer in the mess hall. Beyer was not a man to be trifled with. At night in the compound when no Americans entered, he was as powerful as any general, with the power to make the men obey any command.

"Look at me, Corporal."

Beyer stood just inches away, his head cocked to the side. His gaze was full of disgust. "There are many of us who are worried about you. Make sure you do nothing that endangers your health."

"Yes, First Sergeant."

With that Beyer turned sharply, took his position in front of the company, and marched them toward the mess hall. Kunze waited until Private Ingall was well ahead of him before he ambled toward the infirmary. No matter what else he did today, he must pass the information to the Americans and get out of this camp.

The infirmary was a white, two-story building with a large symbol of the Red Cross painted on the tin roof. It was constructed on the same floor plan as the barracks, except that the interior had been wall boarded to make small examining rooms. Kunze walked in ready to greet Sergeant Olson at the reception desk and was shocked to find a new sergeant sitting there. He was not in corpsman's whites, but the fatigues worn by the military police. The new sergeant was blowing bubbles with his gum, while he listened to loud, twangy music on the radio.

"Name?"

Kunze gave him his name and camp ID number. *"Wo* is Sergeant Olson?"

"Sick, *Krankin,"* the sergeant said, nodding to take a seat on the wooden bench.

Ten other POWs sat on the long wooden bench. Kunze took his place at the end of the line, trying to decide what to do. He stared at the poster of Uncle Sam on the opposite wall, scowling and pointing his finger with the caption: "He needs your blood for our men on the front." Maybe he should just leave. No, that wouldn't work. Private Ingall would surely report it back to the first sergeant. There was no choice but to see the doctor and pass the information to him.

Forty-five minutes later a tall doctor with greased-back black hair, wire-rim glasses, wearing a white medical smock exited one of the examining rooms with his clipboard and called Kunze's name.

Kunze trudged to the room, making sure he kept up a good front. He took a seat on the examining table and fished the paper from his pocket.

"Krankin?" The doctor already had his tongue depressor out, gesturing for Kunze to open his mouth.

Kunze waved his hand to indicate no. "Secret information," Kunze said in broken English, holding the crumpled paper up so the doctor could see it.

The doctor grimaced, then looked more closely at the paper. "This isn't my area. My German isn't good enough to make heads or tails of this. I'll have to go find someone." The doctor reached for the note, but Kunze jerked it back.

"No. For Major Dietrich."

The doctor held up his hands, indicating he understood. "All right, I'll have to go find somebody." He left Kunze sitting on the examining table, indicating that Kunze should stay put and that he would return.

Things were back on track. Major Dietrich would soon have his information, and Kunze would be packing for California. Kunze looked out the window as a horse-drawn wagon left the camp with a load of slop from the mess hall. He smiled. No more pails of slop to carry, no more potatoes to peel in that infernal sweat shop.

A few minutes later the doctor reappeared with Lieutenant Young, the hospital adjutant. Kunze knew that the other men loved to bait Young by giving him the Nazi salute. Young, though not his handler, would surely look favorably on this information. Especially when it contained intelligence about his tormentors.

"So what do we have?" Young was still out of breath from the walk up the stairs, his heavy face red with exertion. He took Kunze's note and studied it for several minutes, all the while nodding his head. It became painfully clear to Kunze that Young couldn't read what the note said.

"For Major Dietrich."

"Dietrich is at Camp Gruber today." Lieutenant Young pocketed the paper. "I'll take care of this. Why don't you head on back to your job."

He'd made a big mistake. Not only had he wasted this visit, but he was unsure whether Young knew the importance of Dietrich receiving the note. "For Dietrich. *Nicht hier* stay." Why wasn't Dietrich here so he could speak German? *"Gehen sie . . ."* Kunze searched desperately for the right word in English. "Go to California."

"You and me both, brother," Lieutenant Young chuckled.

This stupid, white-haired old man was too dumb to realize that Kunze was giving him information to pay back all the slights the Nazis in camp had given him. Kunze realized that he should have bided his time.

Lieutenant Young put his hand on Kunze's shoulder and guided him toward the door. "Don't worry, I'll take care of this."

Kunze left the infirmary and walked slowly back toward the barracks. He had no intention of going to work this morning. Outside Compound One a group of men were building a brick model of the Brandenburg Gate. He wanted to go and kick it to pieces. He never wanted to think about or remember anything about the old country. Germany was why he was in this horrible place.

As he reached the barracks, Kunze started to cool off and consider his options. Dietrich would be in camp again, probably tomorrow. Kunze would simply go to him and announce out loud that he had the information requested and hand him another note. There would be no stupid, interfering lieutenants. Once he was out in the open as an informant, the Americans would have no choice but to transfer him out that day.

Back in his office, Lieutenant Young propped his feet up on his desk and studied the note that Kunze had given him. He recognized some city names and a few surnames, but the rest of it meant nothing.

"Damn it," he muttered.

No one had told him about this Kraut Kunze having information. Hell, this wasn't even his job. It was for the "spooks" in military intelligence. Frankly, all this ratting on the other Germans turned his stomach. From what he could see, the army never got anything useful out it. Most of these Krauts had been out of the war long enough that anything they might know was worthless. Seemed to Young that a handful of the bastards had figured out a way of getting one over on the system. Hell, look at this Kunze. Requesting—hell, demanding—that he be sent to California.

Young looked around his cramped, wooden desk

hemmed in by two big metal file cabinets full of Kraut medical records. He spent his entire day doing nothing but typing out reports on how well a bunch of Nazis were being treated. All this good treatment while Americans were lying in the mud, dying at the hands of these Krauts' buddies.

It was eleven-thirty, almost time for chow. Young looked at the note once more and thought about throwing it away. Finally, he decided he'd better protect his own rear end. If the note had any valuable information, he would give it to the spooks and earn a few points with the major. And if it was worthless, like he suspected, he'd file it in the round file by the desk.

Reluctantly, he picked up his phone. "Heisig, Lieutenant Young. Get your butt up here ASAP. I need you to read something."

Sergeant Heisig, a prisoner who had several degrees from Marburg University and spoke perfect Oxford English, acted as the interpreter for the entire infirmary. Young had a bellyful of him. Day after day the bastard lorded his fancy degrees over Young, acting as if the lieutenant were some kind of moron because he never finished college, letting him know that working in a haberdashery store, making an honest living back in Buffalo, was beneath someone like Heisig. Worse, the son of a bitch constantly let Young know that it was just a matter of time before the Germans won the war and fools like Young would be working for Nazis like Heisig.

A few minutes later Heisig strode into the office, clicked his heels, and stood at attention. Heisig was definitely an Aryan poster boy. Early thirties, light brown hair, angular good looks, piercing brown eyes, and as arrogant as they came.

Young slid the paper across his desk. "What does that say?"

Heisig picked up the note, studied it awhile, then announced, "It says that your women are whores." He smiled politely at Young.

Son of a bitch. Young could feel his forehead flush. This is why he should have gone to the front instead of taking the medical classification on his feet. At least there you could kill these Nazi bastards when you were mad at them.

"Goddamn it, Heisig, I know there's more to it than that. I read the words Hamburg, Frankfurt, Oder. So don't tell me that's what it says."

"You question my German?" Heisig drew in his chin incredulously at the suggestion. He glanced at the note again, then pedantically, as if he were addressing a dull student, said, "One of the men on the train said your women, particularly those married women whose husbands were away from home fighting, were whores. He also says your pilots are no good, that they can't hit Hamburg, Frankfurt, and Oder. He's giving them advice on how they should bomb." Heisig handed the paper back and stood at attention, waiting to be dismissed.

It was just as Young thought, worthless information. One more lousy Kraut trying to get over on the system. He wasn't going to give Heisig any more satisfaction.

"Here," Young said, jabbing the paper back at

Heisig, demanding that he take it. "You tell all the other Krauts that we sure as hell don't need Germans to tell us how to bomb German cities. From what I see in the papers, we're doing a damn good job at it. Most of them are a bunch of dust by now."

Heisig took the paper and slipped it in his pants pocket. "Anything else?"

"Get out."

Heisig clicked his heels, did an about-face, and was gone.

Young closed his eyes and pressed his lips together tightly. He hated losing his temper, but Heisig brought out the worst in him. *Your women are whores.* He should have just thrown the paper in the trash to begin with. No, better that word got back to the snitches so that they wouldn't get anywhere peddling this trash. *Your pilots are no good.* He couldn't see why MI even messed with these snitches.

But an hour later after he came back from chow, Young started to have second thoughts. Technically, he should have turned the paper over to military intelligence, even if it was worthless. What if the snitch who wrote the letter was beaten by his buddies? Couldn't happen, Young reassured himself. Heisig had no idea who'd given him the note. It could have come from any of them. Even in the worse-case scenario, say they eventually figured out who wrote the note, he'd probably be gone. Every snitch Young had seen got his transfer almost the second he asked for it. He was worrying about nothing.

Even so, the thought that something might happen gnawed at Young all afternoon. It got so bad that he started losing his concentration and making mistakes on the report he was typing for the old man. So at three-thirty he called Sergeant Taylor, a buddy from poker, who worked in the records office.

"Bernie, Lieutenant Young, here. Could you do me a favor and see whether this Kraut named"—he looked at the name the reception sergeant gave him—"Johannes Kunze is scheduled to be transferred?"

There was a brief wait before Taylor came back on the phone. "Got it right here, sir. They're shipping him out tomorrow. Sunny California. Camp McDowell."

"Thanks," Young said, then hung up the receiver.

All that worry for nothing. He shook his head. "California." To be so lucky.

5

The Spy Paper

POW Camp, Tonkawa, Oklahoma
November 4, 1943

CORPORAL ACHILLES REHBERGER TROTTED OVER TO
First Sergeant Beyer as he walked toward the barracks. Rehberger's pale blue eyes darted wildly to see
if any of the guards were watching.

"First Sergeant, I must talk to you immediately.
There is something of extreme importance I must
show you."

They started toward the barracks where they could
talk in private, but were stopped when a wagon pulled
by a team of horses clopped by carrying supplies for
the mess hall.

Achilles could no longer hold in his anger and
began whispering about finding the traitor.

Beyer watched the wagon stop and men come out to
unload. He knew the traitor was inside, probably not
working as usual. By checking the outgoing mail
he had determined that it was Kunze who had written
the note offering information. Beyer had compared
the cigarette paper note with a letter Kunze had writ-

51

ten to his wife, and there was no doubt that they matched. Still, Beyer needed hard proof. He could not allow Kunze to claim the note was just an innocuous offer.

Beyer checked inside the barracks to make sure it was empty, and he and Achilles sat on Beyer's bunk. Achilles handed him the letter.

"Heisig received it this morning. Lieutenant Young gave it to him." Achilles shook his head in disbelief. "The lieutenant told him they did not need Germans to tell them how to bomb German cities."

Beyer looked at the handwriting and immediately recognized it as Kunze's. He could not deal with this problem alone; he must involve the other sergeants.

"Go find the platoon sergeants. Tell them to come one every fifteen minutes, so it doesn't seem like we are gathering to start trouble."

Then as Rehberger was at the door, Beyer called, "I know it will be hard. But do not tell any of the men."

Rehberger nodded and clicked his heels. "Yes, First Sergeant."

Beyer picked up the spy paper and slowly read it again. He wanted to be sure he had missed nothing.

Reichs Motor Sports School, drivers' school for all sections of the army, at Frankfurt on the Oder. Hamburg: The main station is camouflaged as a block of houses with dummies and paint; through the middle a wide light strip was marked off as a street. The inner lake was covered over. The outer lake was divided, and an island was marked.

Beyer stopped reading. *Hamburg, main station.* The hair on the back of his neck stood on edge. It was the dream he had been having for weeks about little Edgar under the rubble, his hand clutching the air. The images suddenly swarmed at him. He could think of nothing but going to the mess hall, finding Kunze, and strangling him with his bare hands. In Germany they simply would have taken Kunze out and had him shot for being a traitor. Calm yourself, Beyer told himself. You must know everything the traitor has done. He read on:

Reichsportsanitorium in Lessen. The place may be in Pomerania but also in Mecklenburg. There may possibly be an army munitions plant in the vicinity of Lessen? From what I hear, the chief Sergeant Major, Herbert Richter, wrote an insolent letter; besides, during the train journey here he made insulting remarks and described decent women as prostitutes. With a presumptuous gesture he declared: "Many fields, rich soil, many automobiles, all this will be our colony someday."

The transportation chief of the train, an American captain, had the kindness to give the prisoners a late newspaper. Richter threw the newspaper out the window with the words, "It is poison to our soldiers."

Beyer's anger rose in his throat like nauseating bile. What kind of man betrayed his country, his fellow soldiers, his cities? Even though some of the information was old, it could still be of value to the enemy. If even one innocent man, woman, or child died because of this paper, it was a horrific crime. A man that could do this was no man at all. He was no better than the vermin they threw pots and pans at—the cockroaches, the mice, the rats. And on some level he was worse. A rat was doing only what came naturally; but Kunze (even now to think the name disgusted him) had a choice in this matter. He had chosen to betray his comrades. Though he did not want to, Beyer knew he must read every traitorous word.

One of the new prisoners who arrived today relates that in the camp from which they came a "pastor" took letters from one of the prisoners out for relatives in America, thereby evading the censors. Here they have trucks with high chassis, underneath which a prisoner can hide if he wants to get to the outside.

Please let me write at the hospital if there is something to report. Please inform the sergeants on duty.

Of the prisoners who left today, Otto Hansmann is anti-Nazi. I have informed this man that an American officer may speak to him.

Dachenberger is a rabid Nazi. I do not know what positions he held in the party.

Was it not bad enough that Kunze had turned traitor that he needed to recruit others to do the same? Beyer closed his eyes, trying to find the logic in Kunze's action, other than cowardly self-interest. His mind raced with what to do, who to tell, how best to stop this traitor. Before he did anything, he must be absolutely sure that Kunze had written the paper. He took out the letter to Kunze's wife.

Just as he began reading the other letter, Sergeant Seidel stormed into the barracks. Seidel was a strapping dark-haired man from Hamburg who was Beyer's best platoon sergeant. He was a veteran of the Russian front and North Africa, and had fought in the Hermann Göring Division. He, too, had experienced trouble with Kunze mouthing off.

"Achilles tells me we have found our rat," Seidel said, breathing hard after his trot to the barracks. Beyer wished Seidel had been more discreet. He motioned for him to have a seat on the bunk. Beyer went to his nearby desk and took out a clipboard with a duty roster so they would have a cover if a guard entered the barracks. They must not give the MPs a chance to let the rat escape. Beyer pointed to the spy letter on his bunk.

Seidel leaned close to Beyer so he could read the spy letter, while Beyer read the letter to Kunze's wife. Carefully, Beyer began to read and compare every scrawl of handwriting.

Dear Erna,
    I am well. I am getting older and slower; playing football I am not able to keep up any-

more. The days go by in thinking, once in a while a game of chess, some English lessons, also French. I do not bother about the sequence of the days of the weeks or the date. The companionship of the other prisoners is good. The report, according to the newspapers here, is that Leipzig and Dresden were bombed. I hope you will be spared any misfortune, also in the future, *insa' Allah!* You are permitted to send me books, so will you please? Kant, Jaspers, *Physique and Character,* and chess literature. Regards to the children, parents, brothers, and sisters.

Your Hans

There was no doubt about it. The loopy curls on his capital letters, the long legs that he put on his *j.* The spy paper and the letter to Kunze's wife were the same.

"Look at the letter to his wife," said Beyer.

Seidel held the two notes up and compared them, all the while shaking his head in apparent disbelief.

"I will go and kill him myself right now," Seidel said. He stood up and was clenching his fist. Beyer grabbed him by the shirt and stopped him.

"When I think what this traitor has done," said Seidel, rearing his head toward the ceiling. "He could have already helped kill my wife!"

Beyer knew that Seidel could easily do what he threatened. He was a large man who had done a lot of bar fighting before he came into the army. Beyer had seen him drop a man who had talked back to him with one punch.

"This is too serious for any one of us to handle. We must let all the men know about it, see the letters, and let them judge for themselves. I would like to punish Kunze myself, but we must be careful."

Seidel stared out the barracks door. He was clenching his jaw so hard, Beyer thought he could hear his teeth grinding.

"I am ordering you, Sergeant Seidel. You do nothing. All the men must know."

Seidel continued to look out the door. Finally after a long silence, he said, "I will obey your orders, First Sergeant."

Beyer compared the two papers once more. They were from the same hand. All the men must see this and know of Kunze's treachery. It was only right to have the men teach Kunze a lesson.

"Have the other sergeants bring the company to the mess hall at 2230 hours tonight. We will settle this then."

A hard wind blew out of the northwest, kicking up dust on the soccer field, as the men of Company Four filtered into the mess hall. There was a full moon, but thick clouds scudded past, causing the buildings to throw long, uneven shadows. "A chance of snow," the last guard of the night had said an hour earlier. There would be no more MPs in the compound until morning.

Over two hundred men filled the benches of the mess hall. Many were still yawning after being rousted from bed. Beyer had ordered every man in the company to be present. He wanted Kunze to look into the eyes of those he had betrayed, and see their collective judgment of his cowardice.

Beyer shoved one of the tables next to the serving line so that he was directly in front of the group. His eyes searched for the traitor and finally spotted him sitting at a table at the back of the room near the door. Kunze looked bone white; he seemed to be perspiring heavily.

The rat can run, but we will hunt him down. Sergeant Seidel was sitting near Kunze. He could easily block the door.

Beyer leaped on the table and called for attention. There was a brief murmur, then silence. The only sound was the hum of the iceboxes in the kitchen.

Beyer began to speak, then had to clear his throat. His voice felt pinched, his lungs tight. "Men, there is a matter so grave, so terrible, that I cannot render judgment on it myself. It is an act that hurts me to the bottom of my soul."

Beyer took the spy paper and the letter that Kunze had written to his wife and held them up side by side.

Beyer went on, "I hate to inform you of this, but we have a traitor in our midst."

The men grumbled then as groups began to talk among themselves. The sound grew to a low roar. One of the sergeants finally pounded on the table to regain quiet.

"Come and look for yourselves," said Beyer, beckoning the men forward, "and you will find that Corporal Kunze has been supplying information to the Americans on how to bomb Hamburg and other cities. There is no doubt of it. Look at these two letters."

With that, someone in the back stood and said, "Yes, I know this is true. Just today I received a letter that my family had been killed in the bombing."

Then a whirling blade of voices, fists, plates, and cups began to fly at Kunze.

"That's him, the traitor." Seidel lunged toward Kunze, striking him in the jaw.

Kunze, sweating wildly, staggered to his feet and tried to make it toward the door. "No, no, you have made a mistake. I am not the one." Then Kunze fled to the kitchen and storeroom, and was chased back to the dining area.

But the mob moved closer. A cup hit Kunze in the head, then a plate; more plates until his false teeth were knocked out and skittered across the linoleum. Kunze's strong, squat legs pushed him toward the door, but several men knocked him back into the room.

Zorzi, the priest, jumped up on a table near Kunze, flapping his arms like a windmill. "Please stop beating him, this is not right." He held his head, shouted as loud as he could. "You will kill him."

Kunze stumbled around the circle of men, slipping on his own blood. One of the men edged close enough to loosen Kunze's pants, and they fell to his knees. When he tried to move again, he tripped and fell and the circle kicked wildly at him.

Zorzi was screaming hysterically. "Stop beating him! Stop! Stop!"

"Go to hell!" one of the men yelled at Zorzi.

Fearing for Zorzi's safety, Beyer went to him and pulled at his pant leg. "Father, this is nothing you should be involved in."

"You should stop them, First Sergeant."

Beyer closed his eyes and shook his head. "This is nothing for you to be involved with."

Kunze continued to cry out that they had the wrong man, and somehow managed to get back up on his feet and stumbled toward the door. The mob trailed him, landing blow after blow on his body. Once outside Kunze tripped again and sprawled, facedown, next to the building. Beyer could see the men kicking at his head, turning it into a bloody pulp. They had given him enough. The Americans would have no choice but to get rid of Kunze now.

"Kinder Kinder," Beyer yelled. "You must not kill him or they will surely punish us."

Beyer's voice went unheard. The men were like wild beasts, tearing at their prey. The more Kunze struggled, the more violent the kicks and blows. Someone swung a milk bottle at Kunze's head, cutting a huge gash and knocking him down.

Beyer screamed, "You must stop!"

But his men, if they heard, were not interested in obeying. Beyer had set something in motion that could not be stopped. This was not what he had intended. The point was to teach Kunze a lesson, not to kill him.

Beyer could do no more. He did not plan to be part of a murder. If the others wanted to risk the wrath of the Americans, they were on their own. He walked toward his barracks, sick at heart that he had lost control of his men. He could hear his men finishing off the kill. Kunze no longer yelled; there was just the heavy thud of his body as they threw him, again and again, against the side of the mess hall.

A half hour later a squad of MPs carrying riot shotguns burst into the barracks and began poking the POWs with the butts of their weapons.

"Everybody outside and over to Company Three mess hall," the heavyset sergeant in charge of the detail yelled. *"Raus!"*

The Germans slowly rolled out of their bunks, grousing loudly about losing sleep. Beyer whispered, "Stay calm. Hold fast."

Outside, every barracks was being emptied onto the company street. A thousand German prisoners would be questioned over what had happened in the mess hall. Spotlights on the guard towers swept the assembled groups of prisoners; machine gunners trained their sites behind what the lights illuminated.

The normally cordial American guards were nervous and angry. As Beyer formed his company into ranks, he watched the MPs finger the triggers of their shotguns. The sergeant nearest Beyer repeatedly switched the safety on and off his weapon. Surely, thought Beyer, once they know the truth about what happened, these soldiers will understand.

The guards marched Beyer and his men into Company Three mess hall. Major Polsley, the camp commander, a stout Texan with silvering hair and the bowlegged stance of a cowboy, shouted orders. Polsley turned to his interpreter and told him to keep his explanation simple.

"All right," Polsley said, "a man has been killed tonight. We're sure as hell going to get to the bottom of it. I want ten of you to a table, and I want you standing tall for inspection."

Beyer and his men spread out at the tables as the guards stood by watching their every move. Then Polsley began walking down the rows of men, looking them over from head to toe.

Seidel was the first to be plucked from the ranks. Two burly MPs surrounded him, and one put the cuffs on his wrists. Polsley pointed to the blood on his uniform. So that was the test.

Trying not to seem too obvious, Beyer eyed his own uniform. Khaki shirt, fine. Pants, okay. What was he worrying about? He had not laid a finger on Kunze. *His boots.* There was blood on his boots! He must have stepped in Kunze's blood as he walked out of the mess hall. A prickly dread spread up his spine as he watched the guards lead Seidel out of the mess hall in handcuffs. Soon, MPs had pulled out three others.

Polsley stared at Beyer's boots, then nodded to take him away, too. Before he could even respond, the cuffs were clamped on his wrists and MPs were leading him out of the mess hall to God-knows-where.

The two guards marched Beyer to the hospital, then down an isolated corridor and threw him into a closet-size room. A mattress lay on the floor and took up most of the space. A bucket that was to serve as his latrine rested in the corner.

This treatment was not right. He was a German soldier. The Americans had no right to act this way toward him. He may have wanted Kunze dead, but they could not try a man for merely wanting someone to meet a fate he deserved.

Private Ricky O'Brien stood chest deep in the grave he was digging for the Kraut who had been killed two nights earlier. The red soil was rocky and full of clay, each scoop heavier than the last. Though the weather had turned gray and chilly, O'Brien had worked up a sweat heaving out the soil. He had pitched off his fatigue jacket and rolled up the sleeves on his fatigues. Two other privates sat on the bed of the deuce-and-a-half waiting their turn to dig again.

O'Brien stopped a minute and leaned on his shovel handle. He watched Sergeant Wegner, the NCO in charge of the detail, sneaking back to the truck cab for another drink. It seemed the least the sarge could do was let him have a nip, too. After all, this was the only wake this poor Kraut bastard would get. O'Brien felt a chill coming on, so he began shoveling hard again, only to hit a large rock. A stinger of pain shot up his left arm.

"Damn it," O'Brien muttered, throwing the shovel down in disgust. He hadn't joined the army to dig holes. He could have stayed home in Jersey City and done that for his uncle's plumbing firm. Hell, he wasn't even supposed to be using his back. That was the reason the doc had said he couldn't go to combat.

O'Brien pulled his scrawny body out of the grave. His boots were caked with mud; his fatigues were soiled with red clay. He had the appearance of a miner left too long in the pit—ashy complexion, rheumy blue eyes set in an emaciated face, with curly black hair plastered to his forehead.

"Sarge," O'Brien yelled toward Wegner, who was tucking his pint back under the seat. "How come them Krauts ain't doin' this? I got a bad back."

Wegner reared up quickly, causing his garrison hat to topple off his head. His cheeks were permanently red from a lifetime of boozing. What little hair he had left on the sides was grizzled with gray. Wegner grunted as he reached down and retrieved his cap.

"Major Polsley said them Krauts won't have nothing to do with it." He shut the cab door and hitched his holstered .45 above his beer gut. "If I had my way, the ones that done it would be digging the hole, but the Major says Geneva Convention says we can't make them." Wegner ambled to the bed of the truck. "Jensen, you go finish it."

"Come on, Sarge, I already dug."

"Do it, goddamn it, before I have you on report." Wegner leaned against the truck bed and watched the soccer game that was being played in the camp less than two hundred yards from the grave.

"Look at them," O'Brien said, nodding toward the game. "They ain't got no respect for the dead. And he's one of them."

The POWs cheered wildly as one of the players scored a goal. O'Brien heard "Heil Hitler" shouted from the sidelines. It seemed as if the entire camp had turned out for this game, and no one even noticed that someone was being buried.

"We even tried to give them material to make a Nazi flag for the casket. Their sergeant major told Polesly this guy was a traitor, that he didn't deserve to be buried like a soldier. Shoved the material right back at the major."

O'Brien kicked his boots, one at time, against the truck's tires to remove the mud. "You ask me, they act like they're gonna get away with this. They're acting like there's nothing we can do about it."

Sergeant Wegner sucked on his teeth a minute, while he shook his head. "Nope, somebody is going to pay for this," he said, pointing to the casket in the back of the truck. "You don't pull something like this in the U. S. of A., and get away with it. What I hear is we arrested thirteen of them that had blood on them. We may not get every one of the bastards that did it, but some of them will swing for this."

Ten minutes later, Private Jensen finished digging the grave. The four soldiers carried the wooden casket from the truck, then slowly lowered it into the ground with a set of ropes.

Jensen had been a bugler in basic training, so Sergeant Wegner told him to bring it along and play after Wegner said a few words.

The four men removed their hats. "Lord," intoned Wegner, trying for piety in his voice, "this man was part of the enemy army. Still, from what I was told, he was God-fearing and had a wife and family. We pray that you keep his soul. We pray that you wreak vengeance on the Nazis who done this crime and punish all their kind back in Germany. We pray for a quick end to this war. In Jesus' name. Amen."

"Amen," the other men said.

Jensen played "Taps" slowly, the mournful notes spreading across the prairie back to the camp. It was a sound that made Private O'Brien think of his home in Jersey City and his girlfriend. He found himself involuntarily tearing up. Not for this dead German, but for all that could be lost in this war and how no one would be there to care.

As the bugler played on, the POWs began to sing. At first it was a small group, but soon it grew into a loud chorus. Every one of the POWs had turned and was facing the grave, singing their favorite song, "Marching Toward England."

It's their way of giving Kunze and us the finger, thought O'Brien. They act if as they're not even prisoners. Like they didn't get their rear ends kicked in North Africa. The POWs sang until every note of "Taps" had been played, then went right back to their soccer game.

"All right, let's cover him up," ordered Wegner.

O'Brien grabbed his shovel and furiously pitched dirt at the casket. If he'd been in one of the towers when the singing started, he would have opened up on the Nazi sons of bitches. He could feel hot tears running down his cheeks.

Sergeant Wegner leaned over, his breath sour with the smell of whiskey. "Don't you worry, son. I've been in this man's army a long time. Them Nazi bastards are goners. There's a nice fat rope waiting for every one of their necks."

6

Who Is to Blame

Hospital, Tonkawa POW Camp
November 5, 1943

"BEYER, *UPSTEIGEN*," SHOUTED THE FAT MP SERGEANT IN charge of the detail. Three other MPs stood behind him, their rifles at port arms.

Light suddenly flooded the windowless, closet-size room, causing Beyer to shield his eyes from the glare. He could not remember exactly how many hours he had been isolated. It felt like days. The room was not large enough for him to completely lie down to sleep. He would complain to the commandant. The Red Cross had visited the camp in October, and, the representatives had made it clear that this was not proper treatment.

"*Raus*." The fat sergeant kicked at Beyer's foot. "The Major wants to talk to you."

The light was disorienting, slightly dizzying. Beyer's legs felt rubbery as he pulled himself up off the mattress. He braced his hands against the wall to gain his bearings, and the fat sergeant stepped back and drew his .45 a quarter inch out of his holster.

They are treating me like a common killer, thought Beyer. *Nonsense*. He had not laid a finger on Kunze. It was just a matter of time before the Americans figured out the truth and released him.

With guards to the front, rear, left, and right, Beyer was marched to a small white clapboard cottage that served as Major Polsley's quarters. The sharp, cold wind cut through Beyer's fatigues and stung his face, clearing the cobwebs. Good. He must have all his wits about him when the Americans interrogated him. They would try to trick him into betraying his comrades. Of that much he was certain. He would be ready for them.

Major Polsley was the commandant of the camp. His small quarters had been turned into an interrogation room by removing most of the furniture in the living room and installing a long table and a witness chair. Four American officers, an interpreter, and woman stenographer sat at the table. Beyer walked up to the table and saluted stiffly.

Major Fuller, a gaunt-looking fellow with soft blue eyes and a voice that twanged like a banjo string, seemed to have been assigned the task of asking the questions. He announced that he was a lawyer—the judge advocate from Camp Gruber—and that he would swear Beyer to tell the truth. After administering the oath and informing Beyer that he was not required to answer questions if he didn't want to, Fuller began firing questions through the interpreter.

"Beyer, we want to know what happened in the mess hall on the night of November 4. We want you to tell us the whole truth about what happened and who was involved. We want to know everything."

Beyer nodded and began his explanation. "I called my company together that night because I wanted to show to the other soldiers the traitorous letter written by Kunze."

"You mean the letter to Kunze's wife and the Hamburg note?"

"Yes."

"Go on."

"I said the men should keep their fingers off Kunze and that he would be tried in Germany when he returned. I saw that the crowd was getting angry, and Kunze started to run from them, whereupon the men hit him and the blood started running from his face."

Fuller was asking the next question before the interpreter finished his translation. "Tell us the names of the men who hit Kunze. You were there—you saw it all; we know you know who hit him."

Beyer pondered the question for a long time. They could ask a million times as far as he was concerned. "I sat in the back and Kunze was sitting near the stove, so I couldn't say."

The other officers frowned, but Fuller seemed undeterred. "Then how did you see the blood running from his face?"

"Kunze ran away from the stove in the direction that I was."

Captain Maffitt, the post engineer, took off his wire-rim glasses and locked eyes with Beyer. "We want you to tell us the truth. Names. Don't think you can fool us!"

Beyer shrugged. Let Maffitt yell all he wanted. Beyer would not betray his comrades. "I understand. But I can't give any names as to who hit him because there were so many men around."

"All right, go ahead and tell me what happened next," Fuller resumed.

"Kunze started running toward the door, which was locked, and about twenty soldiers were standing by the door."

"Which door?"

"The entrance to the dining room, sir, the side entrance."

Fuller nodded to continue.

"Kunze kept running around, and seeing that the door was blocked by about twenty men, he ran into the rear of the kitchen. He tried to get out of the rear door of the kitchen."

"Name those twenty men who blocked the door."

Beyer could feel his hands twitch slightly. The stenographer waited for his answer, then her eyes drifted to his hands. He thought he saw a slight smirk.

"I don't know," Beyer answered calmly.

"You're lying, and we want you to tell us the truth. You had better not spend so much time trying to protect others, because we already have information from others, and we want you to tell the truth."

For fifteen minutes they played cat and mouse: Beyer describing Kunze's ordeal in the mess hall, and Fuller demanding the names of those who had hit Kunze. Each time Fuller asked for names, Beyer simply looked him directly in the eye and said he couldn't give names if he didn't know them. Fuller suddenly changed course.

"Did Kunze pass by you?"

"Yes."

Fuller nodded confidently. "Kunze went by and you hit him?"

"No," Beyer said, "this is not true."

"All of the witnesses have said you hit him."

"It is a lie," stammered Beyer. "I didn't hit him."

The question frightened him. Had they scared one of his men into confessing, then promised leniency if he implicated others? Beyer thought back to which men had been pulled out of the mess hall with him. No, even the hothead Seidel would not crack under interrogation. This was just another trick from Fuller.

"Witnesses have said that as Kunze went by, you hit him."

No names, thought Beyer. Fuller was bluffing. "No, it is a lie. I didn't touch him with my hands or my feet."

"Then how did you get blood on your feet?"

"I stepped in blood on the floor."

Major Fuller and Captain Maffitt conferred a moment, and Fuller finally shook his head in agreement.

"When Seidel hit Kunze, did he do it with a board or his feet?"

Beyer almost smiled at Fuller's simple treachery, but managed to keep his stony composure. "I don't know if Seidel hit him—I couldn't distinguish."

Both officers shook their heads in apparent disgust with Beyer. Fuller checked his watch. It was close to lunch.

"We know that you are an intelligent German soldier, and we know it would be impossible for Kunze to have been hit that many times without your seeing someone hit him." Fuller gestured, palm up, as a final invitation to tell all.

"I know now is the time to speak," Beyer said, "but I cannot. I am very sorry, but I cannot tell you anything I haven't seen. Perhaps other people who were closer to him might have seen."

The questioning had lasted for two hours, and they had not forced one betrayal. At this rate they would have to let him go.

A week later Beyer sat in front of the same group of officers. He had been moved to a larger cell but was still isolated from his fellow POWs, so he had no idea what the other men might have revealed about Kunze's death. During the week, he had begun to realize that the Americans were looking to blame someone for what happened. They did not care that Kunze was a traitor. Whatever code these officers lived by, it was different from the one Beyer had been taught in the German Air Force. He began to think that it was a bit of vengeance, too. Many of their friends and relatives were being killed, and here was a chance to even the score.

Major Fuller began the questioning by asking Beyer to examine the spy note again. "Who gave you this note?"

"Heisig, who works in the hospital."

"Did you ever before in your life compare two writings to determine whether they were the same and come to the conclusion that the same person wrote each one? Did you have any training in school in comparing handwriting—are you what we call a handwriting expert?"

"No, I didn't learn that."

Doubt me if you like, thought Beyer. I saw how Kunze reacted, his face turning yellow, then deathly white as the letters were read. Not even his best friend would have doubted that Kunze was the one.

"When you told the men that, in your opinion, both writings were made by the same man, it was clear to you they had great confidence in your judgment, and a lot of them believed it without even examining the writings. Isn't that right?"

"No, the other men came up and compared them."

"What are the names of the men who came up and examined the two writings after you told them that you thought the same man wrote both?

Old tricks.

Beyer sighed loudly. "My thought was that when I finished reading these two letters, how Hamburg would be bombed by American and English fliers, and when a man so foul as this man with a wife and children in Germany, should behave the way he had, I did not notice who came up to compare the papers."

A hateful grin spread over Major Fuller's face. For a full minute he shook his head in seeming amazement. Finally, he looked down at his legal pad and came up with a new line of questioning.

"Beyer, who was it that called the meeting?"

"I did."

"And you knew then that the men would take some

action, including physical violence or disciplinary action, when you took Kunze to this meeting?"

Truthfully: "I did think the men would punish him lightly, but when I read the letters to the men, Kunze became pale and started sweating profusely, and anyone could see that he was a traitor."

"In other words," Fuller said pressing for an admission, "you took Kunze over there, instead of leaving him in his barracks, because you knew that when you read the letter, since you were convinced that he was a traitor, the others would follow your leadership and be convinced also, and therefore do something about it?"

"I certainly did not wish to punish him by slaying him, and I only wanted to make clear to the men what had happened, and my thought was that the men would only administer a light beating on him, and Kunze would eventually be brought to justice in Germany."

The events of that night flooded back to Beyer. His company of men out of control. And then the horrible dull thud of Kunze's body being hurled against the barracks again and again.

"Did you really think there were military secrets in the spy letter?" Fuller's voice was incredulous as he looked at the translation of the note.

"Yes, naturally."

"What? Please tell me."

"About Frankfurt and Hamburg, and a military hospital—that is all military betrayal."

"Didn't you know," Fuller said, squinting his

eyes, "that everybody knew those things months and months ago? How they were camouflaged?"

"No, how should I know it?"

The thought frightened Beyer. Had Kunze been killed over information that was of no use? Or was this just one more trick on Fuller's part, hoping to make Beyer feel guilty? No, it didn't matter. Kunze was a traitor.

"Don't you see?" inquired Fuller. "That stuff has been a matter of common knowledge, and what Kunze would say about it now would reveal no secrets."

"Whether you know those things once, for the first time, or a hundred times, he is still being a traitor."

"And what punishment do they give traitors who do things like this over in Germany?"

"Death."

Could Fuller not see the logic in what his men did? Perhaps they had become carried away, but the justification was there. Would Fuller not have done the same if he had caught a traitor in his midst? Beyer was not so sure now.

"Do you think you and these others will not be tried until you get back to Germany?"

"It is definitely my opinion that you cannot punish us, but that only a German court has the right to punish us. I don't know what a German court will do with me, but it is my opinion that I ought to be judged by a German court, because we are Germans and this is an act among Germans."

Maffitt looked at Fuller as if what Beyer had just

said was completely insane, then mouthed the words, "They're nuts."

"Let me tell you something, First Sergeant." Fuller poked his finger at Beyer. "You are living in America now, and you are going to be governed by our laws, and whenever you commit a crime, you are going to be tried here in this country. Otherwise, you fellows could do anything you wanted down there. We are responsible for every one of you prisoners of war—not just some of you."

"I do not understand the right of it."

For five minutes Fuller took Beyer back through the details of Kunze being chased around the mess hall. Every time Beyer indicated that Kunze had stopped moving, Fuller demanded names of the assailants, to which Beyer feigned lack of knowledge. Then Fuller seemed to turn the moral guilt on Beyer.

"What did you and any of the others do physically to stop that fight and save that man's life?"

"I just shouted, Stop! You must not dirty your hands, but physically I nor any of the other noncoms did anything."

Then with contempt dripping from his voice, Fuller said, "You and the other noncommissioned officers could have surrounded Kunze and kept the others off him, and Kunze would be alive today. Isn't that true?"

"No, I did not wish to do it, and I also did not have the thought of protecting him."

"Neither you nor any of the other men are sorry Kunze is dead, are you?"

Fuller and the other officers on the panel looked as

if they wanted to take Beyer out and shoot him. *Hypocrites.* No *real* soldier would abide a traitor, no matter what they might say seated here judging him now.

Proudly, with his head held high, Beyer said, "I am only sorry that Kunze met his death here. The only other thing I am sorry for is that good people, understanding people, might be punished because of this affair."

7

Revenge of the Holy Ghost

Dallas, Texas
Eighth Service Command Headquarters
November 1943

Colonel Julien C. Hyer, staff judge advocate of the Eighth Service Command, took out the report from the summary court officer in Tonkawa, Oklahoma. It was another German POW camp murder, the second within a month. His best trial lawyer, Lieutenant Colonel Leon Jaworski, sat across from him.

"Damn it, Leon," Hyer said, passing the report over the large oak desk to Jaworski. "Washington thinks this may be one of those *Heilige Geist* murders. Nazis beat one of their own to death in a mess hall full of two hundred men, then the first sergeant of the outfit claims he doesn't know who did it." Hyer took a long drag off his cigarette, the smoke obscuring his beefy face for a moment.

The Germans had a system in the POW camps. Suspected collaborators would be attacked at night, a blanket thrown over their heads so they couldn't identify their assailants, then beaten senseless. Like the Holy Ghost, the attackers were never seen. From what Jaworski had been told, this situation seemed more like a kangaroo court and summary execution.

Jaworski took the file and began skimming statements. He was a small man with graying wavy hair and thick potatoey features that were offset by intense brown eyes. At thirty-eight, he had seen his share of crime scenes. He had gained his courtroom legs defending criminal cases back in Waco. He eventually worked his way into complex litigation in Houston. He already had a reputation as one of the country's finest trial lawyers.

"I bet the 'spooks' blew another one," Jaworski said. The other murder had occurred at Fort Chaffee, Arkansas, after a prisoner had agreed to help the guards, then was not pulled out of the camp. Military intelligence was great at gaining information from Germans, but was not very good at protecting them afterward.

"This one is worse," Hyer said, frowning so his bushy eyebrows formed one line. "The German first sergeant found a note from this Kunze fellow describing how we should bomb military installations. They got him the night before he was supposed to be transferred out to Camp McDowell. The part that is so stupid is that the information he was giving was worthless. We already knew it. The summary court officer thinks Kunze saw pictures in *Life* on how Hamburg was camouflaged and used that. Article is in the file." Hyer ran his hands through his hair and sighed. "We've got to put a stop to this or we're going to have these camps erupting all over the country."

"Why didn't MI have him isolated?" Jaworski asked.

Hyer shrugged. "They claim they didn't know he was compromised. One of the Germans claims he was given the spy note by an American officer in the hospital. It looks like cover-your-ass time to me."

Jaworski studied the crime-scene photos. The victim lay beside a building, his head a bloody pulp, his pants and underwear stripped down to his ankles. It was as if he had been savaged by a pack of hyenas.

The pictures infuriated Jaworski. From childhood on he had been forced to overcompensate for his German/Polish ancestry, for the use of German in their home. During the First World War, his classmates had teased him unmercifully, calling him "Kraut" and "Hiney" and "Hun," acting as if Germans were something less than human. And here once again was evidence of German barbarity.

"What about publicity?" Jaworski asked, closing the file and putting it in his briefcase. "If word of this gets out to the other camps, I suspect we will be seeing plenty more of these. Especially if those Nazi bastards think they can get away with it."

"The commandant at Tonkawa had to release something to the town paper. The rumors were horrible. They had prisoners decapitating one another." Hyer rolled his eyes. He took out another cigarette and lit it. "The townspeople were ready to form a vigilante brigade to prevent escapes. It seems like the situation is back under control. I talked to the judge advocate general this morning, and he sees no problem in keeping the court-martial secret, so long as we have someone there from the Swiss Legation for German Interests. I already have that in motion."

Jaworski pondered Hyer's plan. This case would have to be by the book. The Nazis would eventually be informed about the trial, and Jaworski was sure they would try to use it for propaganda purposes or worse. Americans were being held in German POW camps, and they might eventually be charged with crimes and tried. America had a vested interest in making sure that the Germans' trial was fair.

"Who's been handling the case so far?" Jaworski asked.

"Fuller, camp judge advocate at Camp Gruber."

"I'd like to keep him on the case."

Hyer nodded his approval. "Leon, we need to teach these Nazi SOBs a lesson. The judge advocate general reminded me three times on the phone this morning that we owe a duty to protect prisoners of war under the Geneva Convention. Truthfully, we've been doing a pretty rotten job of it so far. We need to make these Nazis swing."

Earlier in his life Jaworski had opposed the death penalty. His father, a Protestant minister, had considered it murder for even the state to take another man's life. Jaworski was not sure where he stood anymore. The way the Germans had taken the law into their own hands as judge, jury, and executioner disturbed him a great deal. There was a very thin line between chaos and control in the camps, and if a harsh example was not set quickly, he would be trying more of these cases. For once, this might be a case where the death penalty really would work as a deterrent.

Before Kunze's murder, Jaworski had planned to take leave and spend the Thanksgiving holiday with Jeannette and the three children. Now that seemed less certain. He wanted to see if he could get Beyer and the others to write out statements in their own words, so there would be no question about misunderstandings in translations. From the file it seemed that all the German prisoners were willing to talk, but the longer the accused had to think about what they'd done, the more self-serving their statements would become.

So two days before Thanksgiving Jaworski made the long car trip to Tonkawa. When he felt depressed about missing the holiday with his family, he thought about the picture of Kunze's savaged body. Kunze would never enjoy another holiday with his wife and three children. The U.S. Army had failed him. NCOs in Kunze's own military had broken a sacred trust to protect their men and keep order. To allow this action to go unpunished would be licensing the Nazis' subgovernments in the camps.

Winter wheat, so brightly green it hurt the eyes, sprouted in the fields around the camp at Tonkawa, making the barbwire fences and tar-papered buildings seem even bleaker. Jaworski turned the army sedan into the compound, showed his ID to the gate guard, and then drove to the Officers Club, where Major Fuller was holding the final interrogations.

Fuller bounded down the steps of the Officers Club

and pumped Jaworski's hand as he got out of the car. "Lee-awn," he said in his Okie drawl, "I sure am glad you made it."

"Let's hope they're still in a talkative mood," Jaworski said as they hurried in out of the cold.

Jaworski liked Fuller. He'd done a workmanlike job in running the summary court. But he'd been a civil practitioner before the army—mostly land work and estates. It would be easy enough to gain a conviction in front of a panel of military officers. But that wasn't good enough. Guilt would have to be clear to an enemy reader. And there were certain problems with the case. First Sergeant Beyer had not laid a finger on Kunze. Though several men had admitted striking Kunze, there was evidence that the death may have been caused by other unidentified assailants who had repeatedly thrown Kunze's body against the side of the mess hall. Premeditation was weak. He would need a theory that showed a conspiracy to commit the murder or a series of unlawful acts that led to the murder that would allow him to pin it on the five suspects. Most important, he wanted sworn statements from the two NCOs: Seidel and Beyer.

Staff Sergeant Berthold Seidel was a large, dark-haired man with wide shoulders, and striking blue eyes. He strode into the Officers Club flanked by his two MP guards and reported to Jaworski. In fluent German, Jaworski told Seidel to have a seat so they could discuss what happened in the mess hall on November 4th.

Jaworski looked Seidel over, trying to size him up for interrogation. Seidel definitely had the size to kill a man with his bare hands if that were required. He had seen plenty of combat in the infantry, too: Denmark, the Lowlands, Poland, the Russian front, North Africa. From his war records Jaworski had also learned that Seidel was crafty and resourceful. Twice he had escaped from the British, and once from the French before he had been turned over to the Americans. Major Fuller had spent too much time attempting to have Seidel implicate others. It was naive to believe the NCOs in the company would betray one another. Jaworski was more interested in establishing an assault and conspiracy. To get there he would first have to build some rapport.

"I see from your records that you are from Hamburg. Have you heard from your wife and family?"

"No. None of us have received any mail." Seidel sat perfectly straight in the chair, eyeing Jaworski suspiciously.

"I'll make sure to check on that," Jaworski said, jotting a note to himself.

Jaworski sat at a small table directly across from Seidel. He wanted the atmosphere to have the feel of two old friends talking about the war. A *gasthaus* on a Friday evening after a hard week. The Officers' Club bar and pine paneling helped. He had purposely told the sergeant to leave the radio playing softly at the back of the club. Major Fuller and the stenographer, Miss Trummel, sat just within earshot.

His brow knitted in concern, Jaworski asked, "I read in Major Fuller's questions that your home was destroyed. Tell me about that."

Seidel took a deep breath and sighed. A second

telling didn't seem to make it any easier. "I live in Hamburg. I was married on March 22, 1942. My young wife and I moved into our home on March 27. Then on March 28 the bombers came and destroyed our new home. Nothing was left. Our papers, our furniture—everything crumbled to dust."

"Is that why you killed Kunze?" Jaworski leaned forward, nodding his head in sympathy.

"No, no. That is not correct!" Seidel scowled at his old tormentor, Major Fuller. "I did not kill Kunze. I hit him but I did not kill him."

Jaworski held up both hands indicating the mistake. "I'm sorry, that is what the others told me," he said, gesturing with his eyes toward Fuller. "I will make sure it is noted."

Good cop, bad cop.

"Once Beyer read the note on how to bomb Hamburg, how many times did you hit Kunze?"

"Six or seven times in the face, I think." Seidel started to say something, then stopped a minute to compose his thoughts. "You must understand, Colonel, when the first sergeant read the letter and it told how to bomb Hamburg, I became very excited. I could not understand how a man with family in Germany could do such a thing." Seidel closed his eyes while he shook his head in apparent disgust.

"And had Beyer planned this to happen beforehand?"

"No," Seidel said firmly. He seemed to sense where Jaworski was heading. "Beyer showed the letter to all the staff sergeants before the meeting, but we did not discuss what we would do. The men—"

"Did Beyer—"

"Excuse me," Seidel said, holding up a finger to stop. "Beyer should not bear any special blame for this. If he had not called the meeting, one of the other staff sergeants would have been required to do it in order to punish the traitor. No one intended to kill the traitor, only punish him with our fists."

Seidel, like Beyer, was willing to accept the consequences for what they had done individually, not realizing that once they had set the riot in progress they would be legally responsible for the final results.

"Were you there when Kunze was finally killed?"

"I did not do it. As I have told Major Fuller, there was a group of forty or fifty men who followed Kunze outside. I could not see which ones hurled the traitor against the building. All I know is someone said, 'This man is dead.'"

The complacency in Seidel's description infuriated Jaworski. An NCO had stood by and allowed one of his men to be brutally beaten. What kind of odds were forty to one? There would be time for outrage later. He wanted Seidel to keep digging his grave deeper.

"Why didn't you stop the men? You are an NCO. They would have listened."

"In peacetime, yes, but at this time"—Seidel shrugged—"the discipline of all soldiers is not like peacetime. In the company it is not the same, and many times we must shut our eyes. We are good soldiers, but the discipline is not the same. Now when I see something, and give an order, a soldier might say, 'Oh, go along.' And there could not be much discipline in a situation like this. I did not wish that they should not hit him, because I was excited and wanted him to be hit."

There was no remorse in this man at all. Jaworski had represented murderers who eventually confessed and felt horrible guilt. Seidel believed that in this case, it was their duty to kill another soldier. This was what the "Master Race" produced. Now Jaworski was ready to shift gears and let Seidel know he was in trouble.

"I hope you understand that the information in the note was useless. It was too old to be of any military use. Do you understand this?"

Seidel leaned down and pulled up his left pant leg and revealed a long scar. "I am eight years a soldier," he said pointing at the scar. "I was in all the battle fronts, and I have learned from the Russians that little things become important. You have spies. We have spies. One never knows what information may be of use later."

"Maybe so, but I just can't understand why you would take this man out and kill him."

Seidel drew back in his chair. "If the situation were reversed, there would have been many American soldiers who would have done the same thing."

Jaworski hoped not. But he also knew this kind of vigilantism took place in America. As a boy, Jaworski had heard about the Klan pulling a Negro out of jail and lynching him. The Negro had raped and murdered a white woman and probably would have received the death penalty. Yet the people of his town did nothing to stop the mob. Good people who were in his father's church stood by and allowed this horrible act to happen. He had been powerless to stop the evil then, but he had made a vow that he would not allow that kind of ugliness to go unpunished ever again.

"Do you understand you must be governed by our laws as long as you are in this country?"

"For us it is the same as the American soldier?"

Emphatically, "Yes."

Seidel did not answer.

"Do you understand why you are implicated? You are one of those to blame because you helped beat Kunze. You might not have struck the final blow, but your blows contributed to his death. Do you understand?"

From the quizzical look on Seidel's face, it seemed that he had not understood that the Americans could try him.

"I only hope that there will be justice in this thing."

The radio was playing "Don't Sit Under the Apple Tree with Anyone Else but Me." Soon, my friend, thought Jaworski, you will be swinging from an apple tree.

"We want to make sure justice is done, too," Jaworski said. "I would like you to write out what happened in your own words. That will go a long ways toward straightening out this incident."

Seidel nodded that he would.

Jaworski motioned to one of the guards that he wanted to see First Sergeant Beyer. Five minutes later

Beyer stood in front of him looking pale and sickly. He was a man old enough to know what his actions meant that night. He seemed to be suffering guilt over the death, and Jaworski wanted to exploit that.

"Cigarette?" Jaworski asked.

The first sergeant gladly accepted, and greedily inhaled.

"I've just spoken to Sergeant Seidel. He tells me that you are the one who called the meeting in the mess hall on November fourth."

"Once I had the spy note, I knew I must inform the other men and let them decide what to do."

"Didn't you know the men would kill Kunze once they heard from you that he was a traitor."

"I did not think—" Beyer hesitated and looked away a moment. Regaining his composure, he said, "I didn't think the men would kill him. I only thought they would give him a beating with their hands. If I had known what would happen"—Beyer closed his eyes—"I never would have called the meeting."

Jaworski could not help but think that Beyer looked like a wolf—a wolf pretending to be remorseful. How could Beyer not have known that calling two hundred men together in a mess hall and accusing one of their fellow POWs of spying for the Americans would produce a riot, and set off the savage beating.

"Perhaps so, First Sergeant. But once the beating started, you or one of your other NCOs could have stepped in and stopped it."

The first sergeant was quiet for a long time. His eyes seemed to be tearing. Finally he said, "There have been many times that I wished that I had been killed rather than Kunze. If I could put myself in his place right now, I would."

Jaworski had read the statement Beyer had made to Fuller. There had been no remorse then. Kunze had received what he was entitled to. Beyer claimed to have nothing to do with the beating, but he had set the entire ugly beast in motion. They had waited too long in getting to Beyer. No matter, they had his previous statements.

"All right, First Sergeant. I'd liked you to write out in your own words what happened that night."

After supper Jaworski met with Captain Maffitt and Major Fuller. They had enough solid evidence to charge five men: the two NCOs, Beyer and Seidel, and three enlisted men, Hans Demme, Hans Schomer, and Willie Scholz, who had admitted to throwing cups and plates and/or hitting Kunze. Captain Maffitt, head of the summary court read the charges.

Jaworski was not pleased that only five men could be charged. More had taken part in the riot and murder, that was clear. But he also knew they could not look the other way just because they had not apprehended every man who took part in the crime.

First Sergeant Beyer was the first to have the charges read to him. He stood ramrod straight.

"Sergeant Walter Beyer," Maffitt intoned, "it is my duty as summary court officer to read you the charges and specifications in connection with the murder of Johannes Kunze, a prisoner of war under the control of the United States government. You are charged with two offenses. Violation of Article 89 of the

Articles of War, Riot, and violation of Article 92, murder with malice aforethought."

It was at the reading of the second charge that Beyer balked. "Sir, malice aforethought is not true."

Maffitt snapped, "Do you understand what I have just read?"

Beyer's gaze narrowed. Jaworski could see the sweat pouring from his face. "Yes I understand, but the accusations are not right, since I did not do it with malice aforethought. If I had the intention, I would have killed him."

"If you have anything further to say, we will gladly listen or we will listen to any witnesses you care to have speak in your behalf."

"The mess hall was crowded with men," protested Beyer. "I cannot single out any of them, but there should be plenty who saw that I did not incite anything against Kunze. I am accused of killing a man with deliberate aforethought. I cannot see how that accusation can be justified. I almost felt like I should have been in Kunze's place after I heard he was dead."

"You will have legal counsel at your trial who will present your side."

With that Maffitt had the guards led Beyer from the room. Jaworski could see where the first sergeant's defense would be going. No jury would believe that Beyer didn't know what would happen. Of that much, Jaworski was sure.

8

The Defense Lawyer

Guard House, Camp Gruber, Oklahoma
Early January, 1944

FIRST SERGEANT BEYER SAT ON HIS JAILHOUSE BUNK AND composed a letter to his wife. He and the four others accused of murdering Kunze had been moved twenty kilometers south from Camp Tonkawa to Camp Gruber for better security. Beyer wrote:

My Dear Dear Wife Edith, & Edgar:
This was a dreary and pitiful Christmas season. I have thoughts that creep up on me now and make me worry. I have decided it would be better to live on bread and water the rest of my life if I could be free and by your side. How is—

A guard came to the cell and tapped on the door with his nightstick. "Beyer, *Raus.* Your lawyer is here to see you. *Rechstaenwalt.*"

Beyer folded the letter and put it in his pocket. He wondered how they might have found a German lawyer to defend them, then realized that was impossible. Perhaps, it was a fellow soldier who had been a lawyer before the war. No, that would not help. He wouldn't know the American laws and procedures. Beyer pulled himself wearily from his bed. His joints ached each time he lay down on the steel cot. His hands would start twitching, and he could not control it anymore. If he ever made it back to Edith and the boy, what kind of father could he be in this condition?

He placed his hands through the meal slot and was handcuffed, pulled them back through, and waited for the guard to unlock the cell. The guard led him to a small room that contained a large metal desk and chair. A tall American officer stood framed against the barred window. The guard removed Beyer's handcuffs and closed the door.

"Guten Tag," the American officer said in perfect German. "I am Lieutenant Colonel Alfred Petsch." He reached out and shook Beyer's hand. "I've been assigned to defend you in this case."

Petsch was a tall, spindly man with graying brown hair, watery blue eyes, and a long nose. He continuously shifted his weight from leg to leg, which made Beyer think of a crane he had seen once preparing to fly near Lake Zee. Petsch set a thick file on the desk and motioned for Beyer to take a seat. Beyer watched as the file sat precariously on the edge of the table. Petsch tipped his chair back and laced his fingers behind his head. As he did the file dropped from the table, scattering papers over most of the floor.

"Scheisse," Colonel Petsch got down on his hands

93

and knees, and began retrieving the papers. He crammed them back into the file without seeming to care about their order or condition.

Beyer could see his name printed on the file folder. How could this American, part of the enemy, really defend him? Wouldn't he be considered a traitor? Was this all just a trick to confuse him?

"I've read this file pretty carefully," Petsch said, pointing to the disheveled stack of papers. "And I'd say we've got our work cut out for us."

"You do this all the time—defend Germans?"

Petsch grinned. "Well, I try not to make a practice of it, but I've got another one of these cases in Arkansas. But these are the first criminal cases I've ever tried. Back home, I'm just an old country lawyer."

It was reassuring to hear his native tongue again, but the thought of Petsch defending him sent a surge of heat up Beyer's neck. The Americans had charged him with a murder, a murder he did not commit; yet they seemed certain that he was guilty. And now they had sent an officer who knew nothing about defending murder to represent him. How would he even know whether he could trust this man?

"Might as well get started at this." Petsch took out a yellow legal pad and pen. "Why don't you tell me how this all came about. I've read the statements, but sometimes you just need to hear it from the man himself."

Beyer sat in silence for a long time. Could the Americans be tricking him with this in hopes that he might name other Germans involved in the Kunze killing? Was it even possible to mount any defense? The two times he had been court-martialed in the German Air Force the trial had been meaningless. He was charged, and therefore guilty, and must be punished. Why would the Americans be any different? Finally, he decided he had no choice. If he ever wanted to see Edith and the boy again, he must fight, no matter how great the odds or chances.

"I did not kill Kunze," Beyer began, then related the incident about finding the spy letter and the need to reveal the truth to the other soldiers.

"Is there anyone who will claim you struck or kicked or threw things at Kunze?"

"No," Beyer said emphatically. "No one who is telling the truth would say such a thing."

Petsch stroked his chin, jotted down the information. "Can you give me the names of any of your comrades who would back you up on that?"

The Americans—all of them—were always wanting to know more names. He would have to depend on his comrades to use their heads. "Yes, there are many NCOs who will testify not only that I did not touch Kunze, but that I tried to stop the beating. Sergeant Grummel, Sergeant Zeibisch . . . many others. I will make you a list."

"Good, good," Petsch said. "That's one of the ways I plan to defend this case. Show that you had nothing to do with the killing. Seems to me things got out of control and there was nothing you could do about it."

Beyer sighed deeply. "Yes. Once the men started beating Kunze, I would have put my own life in danger to intervene. I screamed at them to stop, that the Americans would punish us if Kunze was hurt badly, but . . ." Beyer shrugged and searched for words. "My men were out of control. This is not like back in the war. They do not always listen now."

"From what I read, this Kunze fellow was fine when he left the mess hall?"

"Yes, he was bleeding from the nose and face. But he ran out of the mess hall."

Petsch slapped the table. "There you go. Seems to me that Kunze met his fate outside of the mess hall. The doctor said his head was split wide open. I believe that happened once Kunze ran outside. What happened outside wasn't done by the same group as inside." Petsch turned his hands up looking for a reply.

"I guess so," Beyer said reluctantly.

"The army is saying Kunze was killed inside. The evidence shows he died outside. The murder was committed by very different people than the army is claiming."

Beyer tried to comprehend where this was going, but his brain clogged with the images of the night of the murder. Kunze being pelted with cups and plates. The grunts and curses as his men slugged and kicked Kunze. And the worst, the sound of Kunze's body being thrown against the mess hall. *A melon splitting open.*

"Are you following me, First Sergeant?"

The first sergeant nodded "yes" even though he did not understand. He had seen so much dying and destruction in North Africa. Before all this, he always thought a man could only have so much bad luck, that if the coin was flipped enough times, eventually it would come out on your side. But when he thought long and hard about this, he knew it was a lie. How many pilots had he seen with their rabbit's foot who never came back. Too many.

Petsch flipped to a new page on his legal pad. "All right. Now, if all that doesn't seem to work, I have one more idea. It's a little bit novel, but I've been thinking about it, and the longer I do, it seems like it might be our best defense." He pulled at his nose trying to scratch it. "If this Kunze was a traitor, which he seems to have been, you fellas had a duty to do something about it. Hell, he was tellin' how to bomb your country, your homes. A lot of that information was about military targets. We have a theory in the law called justifiable homicide. I suspect if you had not done what you'd done, when you got back to Germany after the war, your government might have tried you for treason. We're going to argue there was no choice but to do what you did, if they assumed you are responsible for the beating. What do you think?"

Beyer hesitated, "Yes, it sounds good. Right. But can you do such a thing in American law?"

Petsch shrugged good-naturedly. "We're certainly going to find out."

For the first time since this nightmare began, Beyer saw a small shaft of hope. This lawyer was certainly right about why he felt the need to inform his men of Kunze's treason. But could it really be true that the Americans would allow them this defense?

"So there it is," Petsch said, flipping his legal pad closed. "We're going to use the shotgun approach on them. Put out as many arguments as we can and figure that one of them will hit the target."

Out the window the sky was changing from gray to cobalt. The changing colors reminded Beyer of so many January sunsets in Hamburg: the wind shifting to the northeast, blowing in a winter squall; the big cargo boats sounding their baleful whistles as they steamed into harbor. Despite all of Petsch's fancy theories, Beyer knew he would probably not see a Hamburg sunset for a long, long time.

Colonel Jaworski had just finished his evening meal at the Officers Club at Camp Gruber, when Colonel Petsch poked his head through the door and scanned the crowd.

"Al," Jaworski said, waving Petsch over to his table. "When did you get in?"

Petsch strode to the table and pumped Jaworski's hand. They were both trying the other POW murder case that had occurred in Arkansas.

"Got here this morning. I've been talking to my client," Petsch said. He mopped his hair back and seemed to shake off some of the cold air he just brought inside.

"Take off your coat and have a seat," Jaworski said.

"No, you look like you're gettin' ready to leave."

Jaworski pulled out a chair opposite him. "Not at all. It'll give me an excuse to have some of their pie. I was looking for a reason."

Petsch sat down and stretched out his long limbs. Every time Jaworski saw him, he could not help but think of Ichabod Crane. He also knew that Petsch was a talker. Given the least invitation, Petsch would not be able to keep his strategy to himself. He seemed more intent on convincing the prosecution they were wrong about charging his client than actually winning the case.

"So, Al, you're not going to contest this one are you?" Jaworski motioned for the waitress to come back to his table. Someone was singing "Praise the Lord and Pass the Ammunition" in the bar. The singer had a deep baritone voice with more bravado than ear.

"Leon, I think there might be something to this one." Petsch took the menu, studied it a minute, and ordered the fried chicken. Jaworski asked for apple pie and coffee.

"Looks pretty clear-cut to me, unless I'm missing something. Your clients held a kangaroo court then a summary execution." Jaworski raised his eyebrows quizzically.

"There's where you're wrong," Petsch said, his hands flapping like a bird caught in a trap. "That fellow they killed . . . hell, the man was a traitor. What if one of our POWs in Germany found out that one of his buddies was giving out secrets to the Nazis. And God forbid, he was telling the Krauts how to bomb American positions." Petsch sighed. "What would you expect our boys to do? Let him do it? They are supposed to sit still knowing that this traitorous bastard is providing information that will kill other Americans? By God . . ." Petsch slapped the table, making the candle flutter and bleed wax. Several officers at another table looked their way and smiled at Petsch. "You know they would do something about it, Leon."

"The information was worthless." Jaworski frowned, hoping to egg Petsch on.

"How were they supposed to know that? Besides, the man was still a traitor. Just seems to me that if those boys hadn't done something to Kunze, they would have been tried as traitors when they got back home. It just doesn't seem right that we're calling what they did murder. I'm gonna call it justifiable—"

A young blond waitress brought the pie and Petsch's salad. Jaworski winked at her, and she blushed. "No court is going to accept that argument."

Petsch glanced at the waitress, who had turned bright red. "You forgot my iced tea," he snapped. He picked up his fork and stabbed at the salad. "I realize it may be a little novel, but I think we have a chance with it."

Jaworski smiled. He wanted to goad Petsch just enough to make him determined to use the argument. He was worried about proving intent in this case and Petsch's argument would help. If the Germans argued justifiable homicide, they would be admitting they intended to kill Kunze. Better yet, no panel of officers would listen to this nonsense about a right to kill other prisoners. They knew about the violence in the camps and weren't about to give the green light to Nazis killing people with whom they didn't agree.

"So, what else are you going to argue?"

Petsch was tight-lipped for a while. He chewed his salad like he was working on shoe leather. Finally, he couldn't seem to resist: "I hope you know the murder took place outside. Kunze was fine when he left the mess hall. I think an entirely different group did it."

"Good point," Jaworski said encouragingly.

"And at least for First Sergeant Beyer, he tried to stop the fight. I don't see how you can claim he was one of the murderers."

Jaworski furrowed his brow, pretending to think about this issue. Now he knew exactly what Petsch had in mind for his defense. Petsch was making the worst sort of amateur mistakes. Jaworski had done enough criminal defense work to know that you never gained an acquittal by shotgunning the jury with multiple theories: he wasn't there when it happened, he tried to stop the murder, he was justified in killing the man because he was a traitor. To win, a defense lawyer had to shoot with a rifle. One issue. Admit everything that was extraneous, so it appeared you weren't being an obstructionist.

"Sounds like you've mounted a pretty tough defense."

Petsch wiped his mouth. He smiled like the fox leaving the henhouse. "Jaworski, you're going to have to earn your money on this one.

"Always do," Jaworski said.

Like shooting fish in a barrel, he thought.

9

Cause of Death

Camp Gruber, Oklahoma
January 17, 1944

COLONEL JAWORSKI GATHERED HIS TRIAL NOTEBOOK AND
walked briskly to the courtroom. He was feeling his
usual pretrial butterflies maybe even more than usual
with this case. So many headaches. Washington had
not sent the order to close the trial to the press and
public until yesterday. The POW witnesses had to be
transported from Tonkawa to Camp Gruber under
guard, and they were already late because one of the
vehicles had broken down. Major Fuller had been so
full of nervous energy that he could barely stand still
or quit talking, so Jaworski had put him in charge of
insuring the witnesses arrival.

The courtroom was a long rectangular room with
plaster walls and a high ceiling. Small globed lights
hung from the ceiling by long black wires, providing a
dreary, pale light. A small window on the east wall
offered a partial view of the parade field, but little
else. Two long metal tables, one for the prosecution
and one for the defense, sat directly in front of a

small spectator section. The jury box contained ten captain's chairs for the members of the court. A raised oak bench, to which a witness stand had been attached, was provided for the law member.

Jaworski set his files down on the table closest to the jury and scanned the room. A small, dark-complected man with a thick mustache sat with his briefcase in the rear of the spectator section. He wore an expensive blue pinstripe suit; a large brown fedora sat on the chair beside him. When Jaworski approached, he stood and introduced himself.

"Good day, Colonel. I'm Werner Weingaertner, chief of the Division of German Interests of the Legation of Switzerland." He bowed slightly as he shook Jaworski's hand.

"Leon Jaworski. I'll be the trial counsel." Then he added grandly, "How was the trip, Mr. Ambassador?"

Weingaertner held up both hands. "You flatter me, Colonel. I am merely a diplomat, not an ambassador. To answer your question, the train ride was shall we say, interesting."

It was important to keep Weingaertner happy, feeling important. His report on the fairness of the trial might make all the difference for some American prisoners held overseas, and Jaworski was not above buttering him up a bit to accomplish that purpose.

"I'll make sure Major Fuller puts you in the VIP quarters."

"That is quite all right," Weingaertner assured him. "Major Fuller found adequate accommodations in Blackwell for me. Thank you."

"If we can provide you any information or make your stay more comfortable . . ."

Weingaertner nodded ceremoniously and retook his chair.

At ten o'clock sharp, Jaworski was ready to begin the trial. The eleven members of the panel were in place. Ten of the jurors were seated, and Major Davis, the law officer who ruled on legal issues, had taken the bench. Colonel Elmer Desobry, a West Pointer with thirty years of service, would serve as president of the jury. He was a heavyset man with brush-cut hair and a sour expression. More than anything he wanted to be overseas fighting the Krauts. Instead, he was stuck at a desk at the reclassification center in Dallas. From what Jaworski had been told, Desobry was a man who understood the need for order in the camps. The nine remaining officers—Colonel Charles Gallaher, Lieutenant Colonel Jasper Wright, Lieutenant Colonel Stephen Spleen, Lieutenant Colonel Weston Price, Major Frederick Rohrman, Major Gordon Lupton, Major Clifford Brundage, Major Joseph Crowly, and Major Emmett Jackson—were combat officers who would follow Desobry's lead.

The five accused—Beyer, Seidel, Demme, Schomer, and Scholz—were dressed in olive-drab Afrika Korps uniforms and were seated around the defense table with Colonel Petsch, Major Murray Jones, the assistant defense counsel, and Fredrick Opp, a fellow POW who had been a German lawyer and was acting as an aide for the proceedings. The youngest of the men, Demme, Schomer, and Scholz, looked bewildered and scared. Schomer was thin with thick brown hair and owlish gray eyes. Scholz was short with blond hair and the flatened nose of a boxer. Demme, who looked boyish because of his freckles and blond hair, was a combat veteran who was highly decorated. Seidel huddled with Opp talking about something. But the first sergeant, Walter Beyer, sat ramrod straight and stared straight ahead. His Luftwaffe uniform had been neatly pressed and bore two rows of ribbons. There was a sharpness to his face that Jaworski hoped to portray as cunning. Here was the cold-blooded face of the man who masterminded this murder, he would argue. Here was the face of the *enemy,* the Nazi menace that lurked across the ocean and was killing our boys at this very minute. That was how Jaworski intended to portray Beyer and by association, the other four. If not in words, then in so many gestures and hints.

Jaworski swore in the members of the court, then read the official charges: Violation of the 89th and 92nd Articles of War: riot and premeditated murder. The language of the charges sketched a legalistic picture of that night. "The accused in a violent and tumultuous manner, assembled to disturb the peace . . . and having assembled did unlawfully and riotously assault Johannes Kunze, to the terror and disturbance of the said Johannes Kunze." A melee that turned into a killing. "The accused with malice aforethought, willfully and deliberately, feloniously, unlawfully, and with premeditation did kill one Johannes Kunze, a human being, by striking him with their fists and with instruments unknown." There was the crime in words. But as always, it lacked the emotion that good witnesses would provide. He would get to that quickly, but first he must make certain the record reflected that the Swiss had been notified and that the accused had been informed of their rights.

Jaworski swore in Captain Stephen Farrand of the Provost Marshal's Office in Washington, D.C. Farrand was a thin, dark-haired man, who wore thick wire-rim glasses and had the air of an academic rather than an MP.

"Captain Farrand, is it one of your duties as an officer on duty in the Provost Marshal's Office to give notice to the Swiss Legation?"

"Yes, sir. In that respect the notification which is received from the Service Command is formulated into a letter addressed to the Swiss Legation giving them the essential notification required under Article 60 of the Geneva Convention."

Good, thought Jaworski, as he watched the panel. Everything done by the book. No lingering doubts that the proper authorities have approved.

"This proceeding involves the trial of Walter Beyer, Berthold Seidel, Hans Demme, Hans Schomer, and Willi Scholz charged with rioting and murder. Did you have occasion to give notice to the Legation of Switzerland, Division of German Interests, and did they respond?"

Farrand listened closely, then consulted a small pocket notebook. "Yes, sir, notification was prepared in our office and response was received December 18, 1943, by our officer. Mr. Werner Weingaertner"—Farrand pointed to the spectator section—"the individual sitting in the rear of the courtroom signed acknowledgment as to the date of the trial, names of the accused, and that they were represented by counsel."

Weingaertner nodded in acknowledgment. He seemed more than satisfied with the procedure.

"We call Major Fuller to the stand," Jaworski said the minute Farrand had stepped down. The assistant trial counsel sprang from the counsel table and took his seat.

"State your name, rank, and organization."

"John L. Fuller, Captain, JAG Department, stationed at Camp Gruber, Oklahoma."

"I am wondering what it is, *Major* Fuller, that causes you to want to be reduced to the rank of *captain*."

Fuller blushed bright crimson. "Maybe it's this cold."

The jurors laughed.

Excellent, thought Jaworski. Better to have the prosecution not look too polished. Especially, when Petsch might garner some sympathy with his ineptness.

"Did you have occasion on or about December 28, 1943, to advise each of the accused in this case with respect to their right to defense counsel under Article 62 of the Geneva Convention and of their right to the services of competent interpreters?"

Fuller was ready to answer before the question was finished, but Jaworski held up his hand and cautioned him.

"I first obtained the services of a reporter in the Military Police Section, I mean an interpreter in the Military Police Section, Camp Gruber, and I took a copy of the Geneva Convention with me. I proceeded to the place where these prisoners were confined and called them into a room together, and through my interpreter I read the sections that are contained in the notice I gave them at that time. They told me through the interpreter that they all understood the sections that I read to them. As a matter of fact," Fuller said leaning back confidently, "one of the prisoners—in fact, two of them—understand English. While they don't speak it fluently, they understand it, and they in turn explained it to the others."

That was plenty, thought Jaworski. Fuller was beginning to like being a witness too much. He wanted the prosecution to seem sure of itself, but not cocky. Jaworski took out the signed Right to Counsel forms and had Fuller authenticate them and return to his seat. The preliminaries were over; it was time to paint a picture of how Kunze was killed.

"The prosecution calls Captain W. S. Kilgore, camp surgeon at the Tonkawa Prisoner of War Camp."

Kilgore, a plump little man with a receding brown hairline, looked uncomfortable in his Class-A uniform, as though this might be one of the few times he had actually worn it instead of his doctor's smock.

The belted green coat rode up at his waist, and his khaki shirt pinched at his neck so tightly his medical corps insignia on the collar pointed toward the ceiling.

"Captain Kilgore, did you have occasion to be called to make a medical examination of a prisoner of war on the night of November 4, 1943?"

"I did. I believe it was the night of November 4, at about eleven-fifteen P.M. I entered the POW compound and found a German prisoner of war lying on his left side near the northeast corner of the mess hall of Company Four, Compound 1. His head was lying in a pool of blood. His trousers were drawn down over the hips. The left or the posterior aspect of the skull was impinged against a cement grommet which comprised a part of the foundation of the mess hall of Company Four in Compound 1. The abdomen of this individual was barren. The head, the scalp, and face were covered with blood. The knees of both lower extremities were flexed. Is that all you care for?" he said, looking up from his report.

"Did you later have a chance to examine this person?"

Before Kilgore could answer, Jaworski stopped him. He wanted to allow this scene to sink in a moment.

"I withdraw that question. Let me qualify this man a little bit first."

Colonel Petsch stood. "If it please the court, we admit his qualifications to testify as a medical expert."

Too late, thought Jaworski. Major Davis was already shaking his head no. He wanted this record protected.

"It is suggested that you qualify the witness," Davis instructed.

"Captain Kilgore, you are a medical doctor licensed in Illinois and Nebraska?"

"Yes. I was licensed in 1936."

"And you attended Northwestern University Medical School in Chicago, Illinois?"

"Yes. In addition," Kilgore said, picking up the thread of where Jaworski planned to go, "I took an internship in the City of New York at Kings County Hospital. Following this I was surgeon for the Department of Health at Kings County Hospital, City of New York."

"Did you during that period have occasion to deal with head wounds?"

"Yes. Over a three- or four-year period, I dealt with many head wounds."

"Now, will you tell the court what you were able to determine from the condition of the person that you examined and later learned was Johannes Kunze? Describe for the court the type of wounds, if any, you found upon making your determination."

Kilgore looked to his notes again. He appeared confident. "At about six A.M. on the fifth of November, I called the undertaker at Ponca City myself, who in turn removed the body to Ponca City. The undertaker, his assistant, and I unclothed Johannes Kunze, and I made a complete medical examination."

"Please tell the court the type of wounds you found

on Kunze at the time you made your detailed examination."

"The wounds consisted of multiple lacerations, abrasions, and contusions of the body. Two linear lacerations on the right of mid-sagittal suture line and two on the left sagittal suture line . . ."

Jaworski nodded along as if he were interested. Doctors always needed to show how smart they were before giving an answer in plain English.

"There were numerous subcutaneous ecchymoses in the arm . . ."

"What in your opinion produced Johannes Kunze's death?"

"You mean instrument?"

Kilgore's answer sent a jolt of panic up Jaworski's spine. They had talked about this area before trial, and Jaworski thought they had worked out this issue. At the summary court hearing Doctor Kilgore, in a moment of hyperbole, had said the cuts looked like they'd been made by a meat cleaver. No meat clever had been found. In fact, the only potential weapons seemed to have been cups, plates, and a milk bottle.

"Just generally," Jaworski said cautiously, then added to get him back on track, "according to your medical opinion, from what would you say he died?"

"I would say that Johannes Kunze was beaten. He died of a fractured skull, laceration of the brain, and cerebral hemorrhage."

Back on track. "Is it possible for you to say what particular blow or blows produced his death?"

Kilgore pondered the ceiling for a moment. "I do not know."

The man was maddening. Kilgore may have examined many head wounds, but he could not have testified much, if at all. Jaworski would have to coax the opinions out. He knew this hurt his case, but he needed Kilgore's testimony.

"Could it have been produced by one or more of the blows that you have described to the court?"

"Yes."

Pulling teeth.

"As to the lacerations, the skull lacerations and fractures that you have described to the court . . . In your opinion, Captain, could this broken part of a mess hall cup have produced the fracture and lacerations you have described, if it were brought down on the skull with force?"

"I would say that is possible," answered Kilgore tentatively.

Jaworski marked the cup as a prosecution exhibit.

"Captain Kilgore, in your opinion, could one or more of the blows or wounds have been inflicted by this milk bottle?"

Cautiously, Jaworski retrieved the broken milk bottle from a bushel basket of broken crockery that sat on the prosecution table and held it out to Kilgore, as if he were brandishing a knife. The jagged edges of the bottle were covered with dried brown blood.

Kilgore seemed to recoil a bit in his chair. "I would say it is possible."

Jaworski marked the bottle as a piece of evidence. Each of these pieces of evidence were like accretions on a shell. No one piece was alone enough to prove that the accused had killed Kunze, but together with the trail of blood that was left around the mess hall, they would prove that with sufficient brutality their use as weapons could have killed someone.

"Do you know, Captain Kilgore, whether this type of cup is issued at the mess hall at the prisoner of war camp at Tonkawa?" asked Jaworski, holding up a cup for the doctor to examine.

"Yes they are."

"Did you see any of them in the mess hall on the night in question?"

"Following the incident, I think I was one of the first there to enter the locked mess hall when it was opened. The two tables in the front of the mess hall were covered with dishes and cups. There was a bushel basket setting on the west side of the mess hall, as I remember, near a door, which contained . . . which was filled to one-half of its capacity with bloody, broken dishes and cups."

Jaworski hoisted the basket of broken crockery off his desk and set it noisily in front of Kilgore.

"Captain Kilgore, the dishes in this basket that I am placing before you, are they the dishes that were found there at that time?"

Peering over the witness stand into the basket, Kilgore said, "It appears to be the same basket of broken dishes that I noticed and previously described, which was sitting on the left side, on the west side of the mess hall near the doorway."

One final piece: Jaworski held the picture of

Kunze's mangled body lying outside of the mess hall so that the jury and Kilgore could both see it. Desobry leaned forward, then inhaled deeply.

"Captain Kilgore, you have told the court about finding the deceased, Johannes Kunze, lying against the side of the mess hall. Does this photograph I am handing you correctly reflect the facts as you saw them on the occasion in question?"

"It does."

"No further questions."

After a long break for lunch, Colonel Petsch rose to begin his cross-examination of Doctor Kilgore. Petsch began a slow rehash of where the body was found outside the mess hall, the location of the broken dishes and cups that sat in front of the doctor, and whether he had examined the POWs for bloodstains. All of it seemed to be a beginner's retelling of the facts, boring the jurors. But suddenly Petsch changed course, and Jaworski was wide awake.

"Captain, you testified this morning that these fractures on the skull were so pronounced that you were able to push the bone in with your finger; with pressure you could push the bone?"

"Under two of the lacerations on the right side of the scalp you could visualize the brain."

Visualize the brain. There was something in the scientific language that brought home the viciousness of the attack. Jaworski knew that Petsch planned to claim that the men in the mess hall had only administered a mild beating. It would be difficult to pull it off with this kind of evidence.

"You could visualize the brain . . ." Petsch stopped

POW Camp, Tonkawa, Oklahoma. *(Courtesy Oklahoma Historical Society)*

Walter Beyer when he first entered the German Air Force. *(Photographer unknown, photo courtesy of Edgar Beyer)*

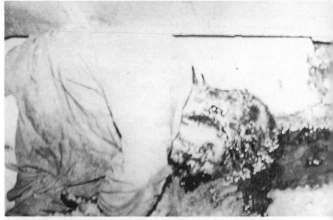

Prosecution Exhibit 10: Close-up of Kunze's savaged body. Light spots are air bubbles that Captain Robinette testified to. *(Photo U.S. Army)*

Prosecution Exhibit 12: Photo of Kunze's body found outside of Mess Hall on the night of the murder. His pants were pulled down so he couldn't run. *(Photo U.S. Army)*

Col. Leon Jaworski (left), pictured in his army uniform, receives medal for his prosecutions during World War II. *(Photo courtesy Baylor University Law School)*

The United States Disciplinary Barracks, Fort Leavenworth, Kansas. "The castle" is where Beyer and the other condemned men waited for the death sentence to be carried out. Beyer was led out the door marked "X" the night of his execution. *(Photo U.S. Army)*

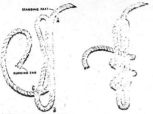

Every detail of the execution was planned. Army Regulation 633-15 even instructed the men on how to tie the noose.
(Photo USD Photo Services)

Length of loops: from A to B should be approximately 18 inches, and from B to Running End should be approximately 35 inches to 108 inches depending upon diameter of the rope. Wrap Running End around for six turns. No extra rope should remain.

Figure 7 ① and ⑤. Hangman's knot.

Tighten loops by pulling at Running End. Lock loops and form knot by pulling down at point D. Slide knot up or down on Standing Part to adjust size of loop.

Figure 7 ⑤ and ④.

AGO 8147B

DO NOT WRITE HERE!
NICHT HIER SCHREIBEN!
NON SCRIVETE QUI!

Last letter written by Walter Beyer, in which he states he is going to the "big army in the sky." Written July 9, 1945.
(Photo USD Photo Services)

MY ADDRESS IS:
MEINE ADRESSE IST WIE FOLGT:
IL MIO INDIRIZZO È:

The United States Disciplinary Barracks at Fort Leavenworth, Kansas. Beyer and the four other accused were hanged in the elevator shaft of an old warehouse. The building is marked with an "X." *(Photo U.S. Army)*

Postcard received by Edith Beyer telling her that Walter had been shot in America. A year later she would be informed by the Red Cross that he had been hanged for murder. *(Photo USD Photo Services)*

A total of fourteen German POWs were executed for murders at different POW camps.

In the above photo the first five headstones are the graves of the Tonkawa camp murderers hanged on July 10, 1945. Headstones face west as a sign of dishonor.

The photos below and on facing page show in more detail the graves of: Walter Beyer, Hans Demme, Willi Scholz, Berthold Seidel, and Hans Schomer.

USDB Military Cemetery, Fort Leavenworth, Kansas.
(All photos by Ed Green)

POW Cemetery, Tonkawa, Oklahoma. Johannes Kunze was originally buried here. In 1946 his body was exhumed and buried at the military cemetery in El Reno, Oklahoma. *(Courtesy Oklahoma Historical Society)*

Grave of Johannes Kunze. Military POW Cemetery, El Reno, Oklahoma. *(Photo Ed Green)*

and seemed to picture this. "And I believe you stated that the brain clearly had been pierced by bone fragments?"

"That's right."

Jaworski had an inkling where this was going and knew that it was a dead end. The doctor did not believe the lethal blows occurred outside the mess hall.

"From your description of the injuries, I take it that one of the three blows, three major blows, on the top right-hand side of the head would have been sufficient to knock a man down to his feet, and probably leave him in a condition that he would not be able to move on farther?"

"I believe that is possible."

Encouraged by the answer, Petsch barked, "In other words, wherever those blows were struck, it is probable that the man fell to his feet, and if he moved after that time, he was carried away from where the blows were struck. Would that be your judgment?"

Kilgore's mouth twitched.

"I would say that it is possible that he was unconscious and carried away, and it is possible that he was not. I don't know."

Petsch smiled and moved toward the witness stand. "Ordinarily, when a man receives a blow as powerful and as effective as the three blows described by you on the top right-hand side of the head of the deceased, ordinarily one of those blows would be sufficient to produce unconsciousness?"

Petsch rocked back on his heels. He grinned as Kilgore tried to straighten out his answer.

"I don't believe that is true—" Kilgore adjusted himself in the chair—"not immediate unconsciousness. It would produce unconsciousness. On the other hand, I don't think that it necessarily holds that any of those blows on the head would produce immediate unconsciousness. But it might have."

Colonel Petsch pursed his lips and shook his hand indicating that he seemed satisfied with this nonanswer, with the confusion that it brought. As he reached the defense table, suddenly he turned and asked, "Now, was there any one of these blows, or any more than one of these blows that you would say was caused by, or might have been caused by, a blunt instrument in the nature of a *meat cleaver?*"

"I don't know what caused the injuries."

"You don't know what caused the injuries?" There was true surprise in Petsch's voice.

"I do not."

Kilgore looked to Jaworski. Jaworski acted as if he was perfectly satisfied with the answers. He could see the jury testing his reaction and planned to give them no reason for concern.

"And of course"—Petsch gestured in a grand theatrical sweep—"that means that you are not prepared to say that any one of these serious injuries were caused by the cup or parts of the cup, which were introduced into evidence, or by the milk bottle?"

"I am not."

Jaworski rose confidently for redirect examination and approached the doctor. He knew that Kilgore had been working long hours with the flu outbreak at the

POW camp. Kilgore had allowed himself to become twisted in his own answer and lack of experience. Jaworski would merely lead him back to the right answer.

"When you say you do not know what produced the injuries, do you mean that you don't know what particular instrument caused the injuries?"

Kilgore took a deep breath, then nodded his head. "That's right. I don't know what instrument produced them."

"You do know, however, that blows of some type produced the injuries?"

"I am positive of that."

Thank God!

Then it was Petsch's turn again. After ascertaining the head wounds could not have been produced by fists, Petsch returned to the finding of blood on the POWs.

"By the way, do you recall how many of the prisoners of war you found in the mess hall had bloodstains on their clothing or bodies?"

"In round numbers, I would say I know."

"How many were there?"

"In round numbers, I would say around sixty."

Jaworski rose again. "Captain Kilgore, did you keep a list of those that you found that had bloodstains?"

"I did not."

"Did you distinguish between bloodstains that appeared to be recent bloodstains and old bloodstains that may have been in existence for some time?"

"Yes, sir," Kilgore said uncertainly.

Jaworski tilted his head slightly to indicate his displeasure. "Did you mean to say that there were as many as sixty men that had recent bloodstains?"

"I would say in round figures"—Kilgore's brow knitted—"I don't know—I would say sixty or less. Maybe there were less; maybe forty. I would say between forty and sixty."

"The matter of keeping a record of those that were found was attended to by someone else, was it not?"

"That is correct."

Finally, thought Jaworski, a straight answer.

10

Place of Death

Camp Gruber, Oklahoma
Court-Martial

KILGORE'S TESTIMONY HAD TURNED A SIMPLE AUTOPSY into a hunt for nonexistent weapons and had covered a third of the assembled Germans with blood; thereby making them potential suspects that weren't on trial. The simple fact was that the physical evidence—broken bottle, cups, and plates—was sufficient to show by what means death had been produced. And the investigators were the best witnesses to show where the murder itself had taken place.

"The prosecution calls Captain Joe H. Robinette, of the Provost Marshal's Office."

Robinette was a tall, thick-set man with oily black hair. His nose was long and set between penetrating dark brown eyes. Even though he had served as a military police investigator for twenty-eight years at many different posts, he still retained his Bronx accent. He was head of security at the Tonkawa POW camp.

After swearing in Robinette and putting him at the

crime scene, Jaworski asked, "When you got to this area, what did you find?"

Robinette cocked his head slightly. "I found a man lying up against the building and a big pool of blood lying alongside him. The man was dead."

"And did you take pictures of the outside of the building, what is prosecution Exhibit 12?" Jaworski handed him the picture of the outside of the mess hall with Kunze's body lying next to the foundation.

"Yes, sir, I did."

Pointing to the picture, Jaworski asked, "Calling your attention to the mess hall building, there appears to be a white spot approximately eight feet from the northeast corner of the building. Will you explain to the court what caused that white spot to show up in the picture."

"Well," Robinette said leaning forward to indicate the exact spot on the photo, "in my investigation that night, there was blood up on that white spot, and it looked like the man's body was thrown up against there and his shoulder struck there and tore that tar paper off."

Now handing Robinette a close-up of Kunze's battered head and body. "Now, in Exhibit 10 there appear to be some peculiar white bubbles, or it looks to be bubbles, sort of surrounding Kunze's head. Do you know what those white marks are that show up in the picture?"

"Yes, sir, air bubbles."

"Air bubbles?"

Jaworski watched as the jurors examined the picture. As it was passed down the line, their faces paled. *Air bubbles.* He suspected they were visualizing Kunze's dying gasp for air as it expired out of the hole in his brain.

"Captain, after you arrived on the scene, what did you personally do, if anything, toward making an investigation to determine what had happened that caused this man Kunze's death?"

Robinette cleared his throat and sat back in his chair. He was an experienced witness who enjoyed being in the courtroom.

"The first thing we done was to get a bunch of MPs in there and confine everybody to their barracks until we could round up all the evidence. We got a milk bottle and a bunch of broken dishes that was inside of the mess hall."

"Where did you get the milk bottle?" Jaworski picked up the bottle and held it up like a knife in the direction of the jury.

"The milk bottle that you have in your hand was laying outside, alongside of his body, and it had some blood and hair on it. The hair isn't on there now. It has fallen off. This is blood on the bottle," he said, pointing to a brown stain near the word "legal" on the quart bottle.

Jaworski picked up the bushel basket full of broken cups and plates and set it down in front of Robinette. "What else did you find in the course of your investigation?"

Robinette looked to the jury. "We found that bushel basket full of broken dishes in the mess hall."

"And on the broken dishes what did you find?"

"We found scrapings from the wall where the man

had been knocked against the wall, where the fight took place."

Petsch rose from his chair, objecting violently. "Just a minute. We are going to ask—we are going to request—we move the court to strike down from the record the statement, 'Scrapings from the wall where the man had been knocked against the wall where the fight took place,' because that is not responsive to any question asked. It is a conclusion."

Major Davis agreed and struck the answer. Jaworski had been a bit sloppy, and Robinette was the kind of prosecution witness who would drive a truck through any opening the prosecutor gave him if it damaged the accused. Painstakingly, Jaworski began taking Robinette through the floor plan of the mess hall to describe where the bloodstains appeared and where the fiber wallboard had been scraped with a shovel to remove bloodstains.

Robinette, with a pointer, began tracing the trail of blood on a floor plan mounted on an easel. "This is the storeroom, back in here we found scraping marks. Along the door that comes in the mess hall, we found blood. Along the windows, we found more blood. There was blood out here on the sink for dishes and in the sink that comes from the kitchen into the dining room."

Jaworski was satisfied. Here was the evidence of a brutal assault in the mess hall. Blood found on the walls and floor and sink; so much blood the POWs had tried to scrape away the evidence. Not the mere nosebleed that the defendants had tried to claim; not the mere blows from the fists that Seidel claimed.

After a brief recess, Petsch began his cross-examination. He examined the mess hall diagram as he was formulating his question.

"Captain, you participated in the examination of a great number of the prisoners of war for the purpose of determining whether they had any blood on their clothes?"

"I did, yes, sir."

"And in the course of that examination you found probably how many of the prisoners of war that had blood, fresh blood, on their clothes?"

"There was five or six."

Petsch looked up from the diagram, his gaze disbelieving. "Just five or six?"

"Something like that, yes, sir."

Jaworski could detect a smirk forming on Robinette's mouth.

"You are positive it couldn't have been something between forty and sixty?"

"I'm pretty sure of that. I don't think there were that many."

His tone mocking now, Petsch asked, "Of course, you are not able to tell how this deceased prisoner got out on the northeast corner of the mess hall?"

"No, sir."

"Did you make any examination of the wounds on top of the prisoner's head?" Petsch made it sound like an indictment.

"Slightly."

Frowning. "You are experienced in the matter of wounds, the effect of blows on the head, are you?"

"No, sir, I am not." Robinette eyed Petsch with

veiled contempt. None of these questions had anything to do with his investigation of the crime, but Petsch was making him sound incompetent for not knowing the answers.

"You are not experienced. Of your own knowledge, you don't know whether any of these wounds in this prisoner's head were of sufficient measure—that is, any one of the three major wounds was sufficient to produce immediate paralysis or unconsciousness?"

While Petsch pontificated for the jury, a sly smile crept over Robinette's face. "His head was busted open, sir."

Major Fuller leaned over to Jaworski and whispered: "He's trying to bate him into exaggerating."

Jaworski shook his head and motioned with his hand for Fuller to be quiet. He needed to listen as carefully as possible to where Petsch was taking Robinette.

"Busted wide open?" Petsch said skeptically.

"Yes, sir. You could see his brains."

Egging him on. "They were spattered out, were they?"

"Yes, sir."

"Approximately how much blood was it you saw there?"

"Two quarts," Robinette said confidently.

Robinette was claiming that Kunze had lost a third of his blood on the ground. There had been nowhere near that much blood lost outside. In his desire to make the killing look more vicious, Robinette was exaggerating beyond belief.

"Let me take another direction for a moment,"

Petsch said returning to counsel table and picking up his legal pad. "In your judgment—I believe you looked at the injuries in the man's head?"

"I did."

"In your judgment, would it have been possible that some of the injuries on the man's head might have been caused by throwing him against this concrete with his head?" Petsch asked, indicating the foundation of the building.

"That was my opinion the first time I examined him. In fact, it still is."

That was it. Jaworski was not going to allow Robinette to speculate about place of death. The killing took place inside, where the accused had admitted to being. He wasn't about to allow this crack in the prosecution's case to open, and have speculation about where different bands of Germans committed the murder.

"Just a moment," Jaworski said, glaring at Robinette to gain his attention. "I think this matter is going entirely too far. This man is not a medical witness. He is entering the field of conjecture, with counsel drawing him into the region of speculation, when obviously the witness is not in a position to testify to those facts. Keep in mind he is not a medical witness. He has testified he did not make an examination of the wounds of the head."

"In reply," Petsch said, obviously pleased with the corner Robinette had backed himself into, "I wish to state that in my opinion the witness has been exceedingly well qualified by the examination presented by government counsel when first presented to the court as an expert, and it is the recollection of counsel for the defense that this witness did examine the wounds on the head of the deceased and testified here concerning the hair which was found on the milk bottle."

Jaworski had not sat down. There was a way out of this mess, and he planned to exploit it immediately. "In order to eliminate argument and save time, may I have the witness on voir dire to see just what the facts are?"

"Just to shorten the record, we will not question the witness anymore. We will turn the witness back to the government."

Jaworski immediately bored in. "Captain, did you make any examination of Kunze's injuries in detail, or did you leave that to the medical officer?"

Robinette glanced down. "I left that to the medical officer."

It was a bitter pill, but Jaworski was going to make him admit all the exaggeration. "In order for you to be able to express any opinion that you would want this court to rely upon, did you or do you not feel that it would take a detailed examination of his injuries?"

Quietly. "It would take a detailed examination."

Jaworski was not done with the public spanking. "Is it your opinion that before you would care to express a view as to the cause of this man's injuries and the manner in which they came about, it would be necessary for you to have more information as to his head injuries than you had at the time you expressed the opinion counsel asked you for?"

"I am not an expert," Robinette said humbly.

"Do you feel you need more information to express an opinion that the court could rely on?"

"I would need more information, yes, sir."

Jaworski had thought that ended the examination, but Petsch rose again.

"Were you acquainted with this accused, Walter Beyer?" Petsch motioned for Beyer to stand up.

"I don't know him very well at all. I didn't come in close contact with him."

Petsch's questioning bothered Jaworski. With a good trial lawyer, Jaworski always knew where he was going and could anticipate questions and objections. With Petsch it was always a crapshoot. His questions could lead anywhere. Many times they did not advance his case. But as Jaworski had just seen, sometimes he stumbled onto a productive area and was able to exploit it.

"Did you know Johannes Kunze during his lifetime?"

"I did not."

Swinging his lanky frame so he faced the jury, Petsch said, "Were you acquainted with his general reputation, whether he was a traitor to his home country?"

Jaworski stood and objected, his voice indignant. "If it pleases the court, that is wholly immaterial. There might have been fifteen traitors, and it would make no difference as far as the issues in this case are concerned. There is no need to interject into the record matters of that kind. We object because it has no materiality."

Petsch had sat down and looked smugly at Jaworski. He seemed convinced this was a brilliant ploy, but was going to allow the assistant defense counsel, Major Jones, to make the argument. Jones, a balding rotund little man, jumped to his feet to speak.

"It is going to be the purpose of the defense," Jones intoned mightily, "to prove that Johannes Kunze was a traitor to his country, and that is the reason why he was assaulted on the night in question here. Therefore, we think with the assurance that we expect to connect it up during the course of the trial, that his general reputation, whether he was a traitor, is admissible."

The jurors stole puzzled looks at one another. Jaworski sighed loudly for their benefit, then said, "A man can be many times a traitor, and it is no justification for the offense of murder. Certainly, it has no place in the record as far as we can see."

Major Jones seemed barely able to contain himself. He looked to be bouncing on his toes like a nervous athlete. He consulted a moment with Petsch.

"It seems that at this time it becomes necessary to make a statement with reference to what the defense expects to prove. We expect to show by competent evidence that at the meeting on the night of November 4 in the mess hall, letters were read by Walter Beyer, one of the accused; that those letters contained damaging information which had been imparted to the American government, to enemies of Germany, with respect to certain defenses, air defenses, in the city of Hamburg, where the wives and children of some of these accused reside; that upon the reading of those inflammatory letters, in the heat of sudden passion and arising from adequate cause and upon sufficient provocation, as we will contend, Kunze was assaulted, an affray occurred. And that reason, and for the further reason that this assault which, accidently, as we will contend, resulted in the death of the deceased, without any intent on the part of the assailants—we are further going to contend, and expect to prove, that it was done in necessary self-defense of country by these accused prisoners of war—in the necessary self-defense of their homes, their families, their wives, and their children. And further, that the deceased, having written those letters, intended to impart the information therein contained to the enemy of Germany; that he was in the act of, and intended to commit, a felony, and that under the law, both military and civil—in both military and civil jurisprudence in this country, they had a right not only to assault him but to kill him, to prevent the commission of that felony."

A wave of relief passed over Jaworski. All the trouble of his past two witnesses had been undone with this statement. It was a cobbled mess on non-law that sealed the five POWs' fates. For starters, the supposed secret information about how to bomb German targets had long been known by American authorities. More importantly, Petsch was conceding that his clients had committed the murder before Jaworski had even proved it. No matter how creatively Petsch tried to stretch the law, self-defense required an immediate danger to that person's life before it was justified to use deadly force. And no amount of speculation about relatives being killed because a note said how to bomb military targets would suffice.

When Jones had finished, Jaworski stood and addressed the jury. "Those are very *enlightening* and *interesting* exposés on the law; but it does not alter the fact that this testimony is not admissible. I don't know whether I am to construe the remarks of counsel to mean the accused did assault this deceased. Certainly, there has been nothing connected up with this matter to bring in such an issue in the case as counsel now presents. The matter of a man's general reputation, a thing of that kind is something that certainly has no place in this case, and as far as I can see, it will have no materiality at any time."

Petsch tipped his chair back and smiled. He obviously believed that he had outmaneuvered Jaworski, so Jaworski bowed slightly as if he were honored.

11

Confessions

Camp Gruber, Oklahoma
January 18, 1944

JAWORSKI HAD ENDED THE PREVIOUS DAY WITH THE
former commandant of the Tonkawa POW Camp,
Major Polsley, retracing the trail of blood in the mess
hall. His testimony had been pleasantly uneventful.
No multiplying numbers of suspects with blood; no
new speculations about what instrument caused
Kunze's death. The groundwork had been laid; now it
was time to connect the five accused with the murder
using their own words. Captain Theodore S. Maffitt,
dressed smartly in his Class-A green jacket and khaki
trousers, was eager to testify.

"Captain Maffitt, did you have occasion to investi-
gate an occurrence of an unusual nature at the prisoner of war camp at Tonkawa on or about November 4,
1943?"

Maffitt straightened his glasses. "Yes, sir, the death
of Johannes Kunze."

"In connection with the investigation of the matter,
did you have occasion to call before you certain

persons to testify as to their knowledge of any facts relating to that occurrence?"

"Yes, sir," Maffitt replied. "The accused: Walter Beyer, Berthold Seidel, Hans Schomer, Hans Demme, and Willi Scholz." As he said each name, Maffitt identified the accused. Beyer, Seidel, and Opps sat at the counsel table, the other three accused sat directly behind Petsch.

"Did these five accused you have just identified give testimony or make any statements with respect to the occurrence you were investigating?"

"Yes, sir, they all testified."

"Before each of these accused gave any testimony, did you give them a warning under Article of War 24 of the Laws of War?"

"Yes, sir," Maffitt said, sounding very official. "I explained that they did not have to testify at all if they didn't want to, but if they did, whatever they said could be used against them."

"And did you use an interpreter, fluent in the German language?"

"Yes, sir. All of my communications with them were through an interpreter. Two interpreters— Private Lader and Private Baruch."

"Did any of the accused at any time indicate to you that they were desirous of writing their versions of what they knew about this occurrence in their own handwriting?"

"Yes, sir, all of the men except Hans Schomer agreed."

Suddenly, Colonel Petsch sprang out of his seat, his

arms flailing in objection. "We desire to interpose an objection to any statements made by any one of the accused while under arrest, while confined as prisoners of war. As we understand it and are ready to prove, they were in what amounted to solitary confinement."

Jaworski planned to put Petsch in his place. "If it please the court, nothing has been offered. There isn't anything before the court, yet. However, in the interest of time, I hope that the court can consider this *speech* as having been made when the proper time does come."

Petsch's nostrils flared. "That's no speech, it was what we think is the proper legal objection. The question, the answer that is being objected to, called for some statements made by some of these accused."

"Objection overruled," the law member stated.

If Petsch intended to claim coercion, Jaworski would delineate every detail of how the statements were obtained—interpreters, the whole works—then have Maffitt retake the stand.

Petsch approached the witness stand silently appraising Maffitt. He did little to hide his displeasure with Maffitt's actions.

"At the time you examined the five accused, Captain, they were examined separately and apart from each other, were they not?"

"Yes, sir."

"And they were kept in solitary confinement?"

"No," Maffitt said while shaking his head. "I wouldn't say they were all in solitary confinement for this reason. Colonel, these rooms were built from cells in the guardhouse. It is possible to communicate from one cell to the other, because the walls are thin and you can hear through the walls—you can yell from one of them to the other, because the walls are thin and you can hear through the walls."

Unfazed, Petsch pushed on. "Captain, according to our information, you examined the witness Beyer, or the accused Beyer six times; the accused Seidel five times, and each of the other accused three times. That is correct, isn't it?"

"Look," Maffitt said, "my whole purpose in bringing these men out, one or a half dozen times, or whatever it took, was to get at the bottom of the case, to get the facts. It wasn't because their former appearance was necessarily unsatisfactory. It was merely our purpose to get all the facts. We operated on the theory that there was always a chance of getting further information out of them, and, to be frank, I believed that they were withholding information from us. We were trying to pry it out of them."

Jaworski was pleased. The jury would only need to hear the accused statements to understand their half truths and myopic knowledge and why Maffitt had to keep at them.

"Now, Captain, do you recall one time when you were questioning the witness Beyer when Major Polsley came into the room and asked . . . started taking charge, and asked the witness Beyer substantially these questions: 'Are you married? Have you a wife and child, and do you expect to see them again?'

Then he asked about Beyer's religion. He wanted to know his religion so that he could have a priest or minister present at the time he was going to be hanged? Do you recall that?"

The jury watched Maffitt for some hesitancy, but none was forthcoming. "No, sir, I have no recollection of Major Polsley making any such statement."

Not relenting, Petsch shook his finger at Maffitt. "It is a fact isn't it, Captain, that in talking to these several accused during the times of these conferences, that in your presence statements were made to the accused by some of the officers present to the effect that unless they told the whole truth, everything they knew about the transaction, they would be severely punished. That is true, isn't it?"

"I don't know that any threats of punishment were made under such circumstances." Maffitt shifted in his chair. His lips were pressed together tightly, seeming to hold back his anger at the accusation. "I will say this, I myself told some of them that I wanted them to get right to brass tacks and rock bottom and tell me the facts in the case. I didn't want anything withheld, and we expected to stay with them and grill them until we got at the bottom of the thing. That was our duty, and that was what we were trying to do."

Jaworski sat a moment and pondered whether to go back through Maffitt's testimony. Finally, he decided there was little choice. The cross-examination had not harmed the prosecution's case, but there was the possibility that Germans reading the record might misinterpret some of the questions to imply coercion.

"Captain Maffitt, you spoke of some of the parties who were called as witnesses before you, including some or all of the accused, as having been in solitary confinement. I wish you would explain to the court what type of solitary confinement that was. It is a term that counsel has used, counsel for the defense, and I would like for you just to state what the nature of that was."

Maffitt fidgeted in his chair. "The solitary confinement that is referred to simply means that each one of these men was placed in a small room in the guardhouse by himself. Now that guardhouse is, the front part of it, is about like this building. The east half of it is divided up into six or eight small rooms. There is a corridor leading down between those rooms. Each one of the rooms I would say would be about seven by eight or nine feet, big enough for a bed and table, and has one window in it which, as I explained a while ago, is a little larger than one of those sashes in these windows. It is a sliding sash opening eight or ten inches to afford ventilation. The doors have a glass panel so that the prisoners can see out and the guard see in. There is a guard stationed in this corridor. They have access to toilets, food is brought over to them from the compound, which they ate, I believe, in their room."

Arching his eyebrows for emphasis, Jaworski asked, "Was it solitary confinement or just segregation?"

"Well, in my opinion it was segregation."

"Were any of them placed on bread and water or anything like that?"

Maffitt grimaced. "No, sir."

"They received their full and regular meals?"

"That is right, and they were taken out at certain times of the day for fresh air and exercise."

So much for Petsch's argument about "solitary confinement," thought Jaworski.

"Now, Captain Maffitt. You spoke of having examined any witnesses that were brought before you for perhaps as long as an hour and a half, or two hours, or even three hours. Do you believe the examination was one that was impeded in any way and slowed any by reason of having to use interpreters?"

Jaworski watched the jurors take a few notes. He seemed to be crossing off their concerns one at a time.

"Oh, it sure was," Maffitt answered enthusiastically, catching the drift of Jaworski's questions. "I would have to ask the question, the interpreter would have to frame that in German and pass it to the prisoner, and the prisoner a lot of the times would have to talk back and forth with the interpreter. Maybe there was five times as much conversation between the prisoner and the interpreter as between me and the interpreter in order to get the idea over to them and then translated into English and taken down by the reporter. That naturally slowed the whole proceeding down."

"Did you find it necessary to recall some of the witnesses because of testimony given by other witnesses subsequent to the time they were first interrogated?"

"Yes, that is true. In an investigation of this sort,

where there are so many people to interview and so many different angles to it, it was naturally a very slow and tedious process."

Matter closed, thought Jaworski. No one reading the record could claim that the interrogations were improper.

After lunch Jaworski prepared to call the interpreters. Their testimony was a necessary link in offering the statements of the accused as well as reassuring the jury that Beyer and the other men knew the consequences of freely answering questions.

The first witness was Private Kurt H. Baruch. He and his family had fled Hamburg five years earlier. Though he spoke with a pronounced German accent, his English was perfect. His face still had the acned look of a teenager, with a large sharp nose set between soft blue eyes. He took the stand with the gangly walk of a boy. Jaworski took him through his competency to speak English and German, then focused on the interrogations.

"Did you serve as an interpreter when a number of witnesses were called before Captain Maffitt to relate the facts within their knowledge as to the occurrence involving the death of Johannes Kunze."

"I did, sir."

"Were the accused, Walter Beyer, Berthold Seidel, Hans Schomer, Hans Demme, and Willi Scholz among the number?"

Baruch rung his hat in his hands. "That's right, sir."

"Did you correctly interpret from the English language to German and vice versa?"

"I did, sir."

"Do you recall whether or not any warnings were given to each of the witnesses that appeared before Captain Maffitt prior to their giving any testimony?"

"Yes, sir."

"Tell us what it was, please?"

Baruch sat up straight and looked at the jury. "The accused were warned that they did not have to make any statements which could be used against them before a court, but that any statements they made would eventually be used against them."

"Was that warning given only one time, or was it given several times?"

"Several times."

"During the interrogation of *any* of the witnesses, were they at any time threatened?"

"Just a moment," Petsch said, objecting loudly. "If it please the court, the question is clearly leading and suggestive, and we object to it on that grounds."

Petsch never seemed to miss a chance to emphasize matters that were to his clients' detriment. "I believe I asked him to state whether or not any of the witnesses were threatened. I don't know that there is anything suggestive about that."

"The objection is overruled," the law member said. "The witness may proceed."

"No, they were not."

"Your witness," Jaworski said.

After more wrangling about Baruch's translating only what the officers asked, Petsch took his cross-examination on a different tact.

"How old are you?"

139

"Twenty-one years old, sir."

"Where were you born?"

"In Hamburg, Germany."

"How long have you been in this country?"

"Five years, sir."

"What is your religious affiliation?"

Baruch paused, glanced at this feet. "Jewish, sir."

With annoyance on his face, Jaworski said, "Just a moment. I don't think that has any connection."

Though this was causing Baruch some pain, Jaworski could not have asked for a better question to help the prosecution. None of the accused were members of the Nazi party, but Jaworski had been looking for a means to introduce the taint of Hitler's racial policies. And here it was being offered by the defense.

Petsch said, "If it does not have any bearing, that is of course for the court. That's all."

Jaworski thought of not asking any more questions, allowing the damage of Petsch's racism to sink in. But the sight of Baruch, head down, a flush of embarrassment still on his cheeks, stirred some anger in Jaworski. The same feeling he'd had as a child when he'd been mocked for speaking German.

"Are you an American citizen?"

Baruch lifted his head proudly. "Yes, sir."

"When did your American citizenship become complete?"

"On January 7, I believe it was, this year."

"Have you been used as one of the official interpreters by the commanding officer of the prisoner of war camp at Tonkawa?"

"Yes, sir."

Jaworski turned and shook his head at Petsch. Several members of the jury frowned in apparent displeasure. "The prosecution has no further questions."

The confessions of the accused were the nugget that Jaworski wanted to lay in front of the jury, but that could not be done instantly. Step after tedious step would have to be made in order to accomplish that. First the interpreters must attest to the proper translation, then Miss Wilma Trummel must testify that she had transcribed the testimony accurately, and finally Maffitt must be put back on the stand to introduce the documents that had been transcribed. At last, Maffitt held the first of four confessions in his hand and was ready to testify.

"Captain Maffitt, I ask you to examine this instrument and tell the court what it purports to be?"

"This is the transcript of the testimony given by Hans Demme in the hearing of the summary court into the matter of Kunze's death."

Jaworski handed the transcript to the law member. "The prosecution offers into evidence the instrument just identified by the witness as prosecution Exhibit 18."

"To which we object," Major Jones said. "The objection is that the very nature of the circumstances under which this statement was secured means it cannot be voluntary. It cannot be of such a voluntary nature as will meet the requirements of the law and of Article of War 24 with respect to self-incriminating statements. The predicate has already shown that threats were made against these accused; that they

141

were 'grilled,' according to the testimony of Captain Maffitt, and that the whole situation and the whole procedure was not only a summary court investigation but a summary investigation somewhat in the nature, according to his testimony, of a star chamber proceeding. Five or six statements were taken from these accused for the purpose of compelling them to confess."

Major Jones proceeded to cite legal precedent on involuntary confessions not being admissible into evidence. Jaworski listened calmly, knowing that Maffitt and the interpreters had already protected the record. Then Jones took a new direction. He asked that the court first rule on the voluntariness issue before the defense would decide whether to put on Hans Demme. Jaworski saw a wonderful opportunity. He had been unsure whether any of the defendants would testify, and now he was being given a chance to cross-examine one of them, even if on a limited issue.

"I think counsel ought not to trifle with the rulings of the court," Jaworski said, trying to prod Jones into putting Demme on the stand out of anger. "If he wants to put the accused on the witness stand at this time, we have no objection. As a matter of fact, we think it is his right to do it."

Jones whispered something to Petsch, at which Petsch looked concerned. Petsch held up his hands in a gesture that seemed to say, "Do what you think is best."

"The defense calls Hans Demme."

Sergeant Hans Demme was a slight, blond man with a boyish face. Although he was twenty-three and had seen combat in Russia and five other countries, his demeanor was still that of a teenager. He took the stand and was administered the oath. He seemed baffled and in awe that he was facing these charges.

His face did not look like that of a killer, but Jaworski knew better. He had spent many hours reading Demme's statement and talking to Maffitt about the German's testimony.

"Showed no remorse," Maffitt had explained.

The MPs had arrested Demme because his uniform was covered in fresh blood. When Demme was asked how this occurred, he freely answered to Maffitt, "I am not strong, sir, but I gave it to him just the same." Then Maffitt had demonstrated how Demme had wound up his fist and smashed Kunze in the face.

Demme's uniform had become soiled when he single-handedly dived on Kunze and kept him from escaping out the door to summon help. Demme had pulled him back into the pack of wild men in the dining hall to be savaged.

Most importantly, Demme had admitted to helping kill Kunze. While Maffitt had been unable to persuade any of the others to take the plunge, Demme had nonchalantly admitted his role when Maffitt asked, "Do you think you helped kill him?" And Demme had said proudly, "Yes, sir, I think so."

Now that his lawyers had told him how damaging those admissions were, Jaworski could see why Demme wanted out of them. Fortunately, Jaworski knew that military jurors had seen plenty of after-the-fact regrets and recantations.

Petsch, in his most fatherly voice, began the questioning. "Did you, after the fourth day of November, 1943, appear before Captain Maffitt a number of times for questioning?"

Softly he said, "Yes, sir."

"Before you came into the presence of Captain Maffitt were you with the other prisoners of war or were you kept at some other place?"

"I was kept by myself, sir, under arrest. In solitary confinement." Demme stared wide-eyed around the room.

Just a little too coached, thought Jaworski.

"How many times, to your recollection, did you appear before Captain Maffitt for questioning in connection with the death of Johannes Kunze?

"Three times."

"Did you understand anything of what Captain Maffitt said to you excepting to the extent that the interpreter translated it?"

"No, sir," Demme said.

"Were you told by the translator at any time that you appeared before Captain Maffitt anything to the effect that you did not have to give any testimony or make any statements?"

"No," Demme said, then added without being asked, "I was told I had to answer."

Petsch returned to the counsel table and picked up a written statement. "After one of these conferences with Captain Maffitt, did you make a written statement of the facts as to what happened on the night of November 4, 1943?"

Already anticipating where he was going, Demme answered, "Yes, but I was told that I had to."

Jaworski remained seated a moment, trying to raise Demme's apprehension. Suddenly he asked, "Do I understand correctly that you said you did not understand the interpreter when you answered the questions propounded by Captain Maffitt?"

Still wide-eyed, Demme said, "I understood the interpreter. When I do not understand him, I ask him again."

Raising from his chair, an open scowl of disbelief on his face, Jaworski asked, "Did I understand you to say that the interpreter told you that you *had* to answer the questions that were asked of you?"

He gave the same script. "I had to answer the questions."

Now in rapid fire, Jaworski asked, "Which questions?"

Demme looked to his counsel table. "Almost all questions."

"Just what exactly did the interpreter say?"

"I cannot repeat that exactly." Once again he looked to Petsch. Demme's expression was clearly "is that right, is this what I should be saying?"

Petsch started to say something, then sighed deeply.

"Were you asked to tell the truth?"

"Yes."

"Did you tell the truth?"

"Yes."

"Did the interpreter ask you to tell only the truth?"

"Yes," Demme said sullenly.

Jaworski sensed he had Demme. His memory was too conveniently blank on the issues that really mattered.

"And when you wrote the statement for Captain Maffitt, in your own hand, in your own words, that was the truth as well, wasn't it?"

"Yes," Demme said. His voice sounded defeated.

Major Jones and Colonel Petsch argued vociferously that the statement was not made voluntarily. Nonetheless, the law member allowed Hans Demme's handwritten statement into evidence. Jaworski made a mental mark in his mind, one down, four to go.

The next day Petsch made the same argument to exclude the confessions of Seidel, Schomer, Scholz, and Beyer. Though not as damning as Demme's statement, each contained a damaging admission. Seidel and Scholz admitted striking Kunze hard. Beyer conceded that he had called the meeting. With each statement the law member ruled they were admissible, and their excuses for answering tumbled like so many dominoes.

12

Auslanders and Lies

Camp Gruber, Oklahoma
January 19, 1944

WALTER BEYER WATCHED PETSCH CONFER WITH THE prosecutor, Colonel Jaworski. They should be enemies, thought Beyer, unwilling to acknowledge the other's presence. Yet Petsch seemed to be on friendly terms with the enemy. Jaworski had his hand on Petsch's shoulder, and they were both chuckling about something. Frederick Opp, the German POW who had been a German lawyer and sat at the defense table to act as an adviser, tried to explain that the American system of justice was different from the German, that American lawyers fought hard in the courtroom, but could be friends afterward. It was just one more thing that seemed alien about the whole process. Beyer understood the seriousness of the charges, and he could not fathom why the Americans refused to see the justice in what happened to Kunze; surely if they had been in his position, they would have done the same thing?

When the guards escorted Beyer to the courtroom

that morning, he had seen the next witness slumped on a bench at the end of the hall: the *Auslander,* Joseph Heidutzek, a draftee who had first served in the Polish Army and hated Germans. Schomer had reported many verbal fights during kitchen work with Heidutzek. Heidutzek, like Kunze, was one of those men who thought he was too good to work.

The law member called the court to order, and Jaworski summoned the *Auslander.* Heidutzek, a tall gaunt man with thick black hair, swept into the courtroom still wearing his long gray field coat. To Beyer, he looked like the grim reaper coming to pay a visit.

Jaworski took the witness through the preliminaries of that night, then placed him at the scene of Kunze's assault. "Will you state in substance what First Sergeant Beyer said at that meeting?

Heidutzek refused to look at the defendants. Instead, he turned toward the American officers in the jury box. "It was about nine o'clock, and First Sergeant Beyer asked for silence, then read a letter which Kunze had written concerning Hamburg . . . a note which Kunze had written and had given to the Americans. An American had given that note back to Beyer and had said, 'What kind of swine have you in your company?' "

"Is this the letter?" Jaworski showed the spy letter to Heiduztek.

"Yes.

"After Beyer had showed the letter to the men, did you see anyone strike Kunze?"

"At least five or six men," he answered eagerly, "but

148

I only knew a few. I don't know the others." His brow knitted in concentration, then he added. "I am sure of Sergeant Seidel. I also saw Sergeant Schomer throw two cups at Kunze."

"Did you at any time that night have occasion to observe Seidel's hands?"

"Yes," he said, holding his hands out to the jury and fluttering them like nervous birds. "They were full of blood."

Asking questions more quickly, Jaworski said, "Did Kunze ever cry out that evening?"

"No."

"Did Beyer," Jaworski pointed an accusatory finger at him, "make any effort to stop the beating?"

"No. There was only a priest or a minister who said 'Stop' and told them to cease, and he came twice and told them to cease. Beyer said nothing."

"Turn around and tell the court if you see Beyer in this room."

His great gray field coat dragged the floor as he turned. The *Auslander*'s eyes would only meet Beyer's for a second, before he focused on Seidel at the end of the table. "No, I do not see him. Yes, there he is." He pointed to Beyer.

Was the *Auslander* deaf? Did he not hear Beyer yelling at the men to stop the beating? Beyer could not believe that this man was allowed to say such things.

The court took a long recess, then it was Colonel Petsch's turn to deal with the *Auslander*. Beyer and the other four accused had described Heidutzek's hatred of Germans, and Petsch assured them that he would "teach" this man a lesson.

Petsch rose from the counsel table and eyed Heidutzek for a long time before his first question.

"It is true, is it not, that your first service in the army was in the *Polish* Army?"

"Yes."

"And you were captured by the Germans on September 12, 1939?"

"Yes."

"And at that time many of the soldiers in your company, on your side, were killed?"

"Yes," Heidutzek answered reluctantly.

"And at the time that you were captured by the Germans, you felt very bitter toward them, did you not?"

"Yes."

"And you worked in the kitchen with Sergeant Schomer," he said pointing to the stocky man beside Seidel.

Refusing to look at the accused, he said, "Yes."

"And you and Sergeant Schomer, during the time that you have been working in the kitchen together, for at least two months before Kunze was killed, had many arguments?"

Heidutzek pondered the question a moment, then shook his head. "We worked mostly together."

Pressing the issue further, he said, "But it is true that you and Schomer had many arguments?"

"Yes, at times, but very seldom, very little."

Petsch arched his eyebrows in a show for the jury to see. If they noticed, Beyer could not see any reaction from them. "You remember the time when you told Schomer that someday you would do something to him that he would remember for the balance of his life?"

"We have never talked such things. Such things did not happen with us."

"Do you mean to say that you and Sergeant Schomer are good friends?"

"Yes, we are friends. There was a comradeship. We had to work together, and there has to be comradeship to work in the kitchen."

Schomer rolled his eyes at Beyer. They had talked about the need to punish Heidutzek several times for his back talk in the kitchen. Schomer had wanted to box the man's ears on the spot, and now they were "best of friends." It was obvious that the American prosecutor would have people say anything.

Petsch was about to sit down, when Fuller grabbed his sleeve and whispered a question.

"Oh, yes, one more question. You don't know whether the two cups which you saw Schomer throw hit Kunze or not, do you?"

"No, I cannot say that. I did not see it."

With that the *Auslander* stood and left the courtroom. Beyer could only wonder what favors the Americans had promised to have him testify.

The next day, Jaworski had two Germans waiting to testify: Georg Person and the "priest," Zorzi. From the previous day's testimony, Beyer was certain they would have a slant on the events of the night of November 4 that was either biased or inaccurate. Person, a man Beyer's age, should have known better than to betray his comrades.

After taking Person through the reading of the note

and the start of the brawl, Jaworski centered in on Beyer's actions.

"Did Sergeant Beyer make any effort to stop the beating while it was in progress?"

Person was a small man who had always looked older than his thirty-four years. He jaw was already jowly, and what brown hair he had left was quickly receding. Beyer had always found him shifty and unwilling to look him in the eye. Beyer was sure Person held some grudge against the five of them.

"I did not see anything of that," he said, looking down at his feet.

"Did you see anyone attempt to stop the beating and if so, who was it?"

"Zorzi, the Catholic priest."

"What did Zorzi say?"

"He said," Person looked at Beyer, "they should stop and that it was a sin. Then Sergeant Beyer said to him that this was no place for him, he should leave."

So that was it, thought Beyer. *Religion.*

"Beyer said that to Zorzi?" Jaworski asked again.

Now glaring at all the accused. "Zorzi said it was a sin, and it wasn't only Beyer, there were several others who said that Zorzi should leave and that it was no place for him, that he had no business there."

Beyer stopped listening to the testimony. Person had no intention of informing the Americans of how Beyer had tried to stop the men. Touching Kunze was a "sin" and that was that. But what of Kunze's "sin" in killing women and children by telling the Americans how to bomb Hamburg? Somehow the Americans were not interested in that!

"The prosecution calls Victor Zorzi." The "priest" took the witness stand, and Beyer prepared for the worst. More sin, more judgment. But the pale, red-haired ghostly figure claimed that he could not remember much of anything specific. Finally, after much prying, Jaworski asked whether Beyer had told him to leave the mess hall.

"I can't remember the exact words which he said to me, but he was excited and made helpless gestures with his hands and then told me to go outside."

"When you went outside where did you go?"

"I went to the church barracks, that was the barracks which was for the purpose of religious services. There were two rooms there, and that is where I usually am during the daytime."

"When you were leaving did you call out anything to the men assembled there?"

"I don't recall exactly, but the general words were approximately that the whole thing would have bad consequences."

Finally, one of the prosecution witnesses was being honest, thought Beyer. No script of fantasy, no embellishment to please the Americans.

"What consequences?"

"That is hard to say, what excited me very much is hard to say. I foresaw that the man who was the traitor would probably be beaten. It was the instinctive feeling that in a case such as this the sad position of the prisoner of war manifests itself," Zorzi sighed in exasperation. "One knows for sure that such a man in the home country will be executed."

Couldn't the Americans see? Even the priest spoke

the truth about Kunze. He was a traitor. Beyer and his men were under a duty to do something about such a man.

"Did Sergeant Beyer, in your presence, after reading from a note or conferring with noncommissioned officers, make any attempt to quiet the meeting and restore order?"

Zorzi looked to Beyer. It was a look of helplessness, a look saying "please forgive me."

"At that particular moment I didn't hear anything, but later on when I asked Sergeant Beyer whether he had given consideration to this matter, Sergeant Beyer's voice was not very loud, but he said, he made some statement to the effect: 'Men consider this well, the Americans can make difficulties for you in this matter.' At that particular moment it is likely that it was impossible to stop the excitement, since in each individual man there was such an excitement that it would have been impossible for any one voice to pierce the commotion."

What Zorzi said was the truth. Beyer could not have stopped his men, even if he'd possessed a gun. They had turned into something that he did not recognize. Beyer had never intended for Kunze to be killed. A beating, yes. A bad beating that would have required the Americans to get the traitor out of their midst, but not murder.

Beyer thought that was all the Americans planned to present, but before they were to recess that day, Jaworski had the other prosecutor, Major Fuller, retake the stand and look at a magazine.

"Major Fuller, are you acquainted with the publication that is known as *Life Magazine?*"

"I am. It is a weekly periodical containing news items and other matters of general circulation. It is one of the most popular magazines that appears at the newsstands in the United States."

Jaworski handed Fuller the magazine open in the middle to pictures. "I will ask you to take a look at this magazine and state whether it is one of the issues of *Life Magazine.*"

Fuller looked at the magazine. "It is."

"What is the date?"

"Its date is August 4, 1941."

"Is there a page in that magazine relating to the camouflage of installations at Hamburg, Germany?"

"Yes, sir."

Petsch rose and loudly objected. "Just a minute. There is no evidence here to show that at the time of the publication of the magazine, or at any time thereafter any one of these defendants had any knowledge of the publication of the facts therein set forth. There is nothing here to show they participated in the publication; nothing here to show that they read the publication; nothing here to show that somebody else read it to them; nothing here to show that it was available to them, or that they ever saw it; and therefore, it may have been a matter of general knowledge to the public in America, certainly it could not be considered a matter of general knowledge to the public in Germany or the German armies on the Russian front or in Africa. There is nothing to show that they ever saw that magazine."

Beyer strained to see the picture. No one had ever shown him this photo, but he was not sure he wanted to see more pictures of his bombed city. Frankly, it did not matter. Kunze had offered to be a traitor. As Seidel had said many times, "It was the little things that cost the great defeat in Russia." If Kunze's treachery added one scrap of knowledge to the Americans, it was still a crime, regardless of how the Americans might minimize it.

After a long period of wrangling, the military judge admitted the pictures. They were done for the day.

13

Spy Handlers

THE TONKAWA INTELLIGENCE OFFICERS HAD INFORMED Jaworski that Colonel Petsch and Major Fuller had been poking around, asking questions that would establish that Kunze had been a spy since his arrival at the POW camp. It was clear to Jaworski that military intelligence had handled Kunze badly. He never should have been left in the camp for so long, especially when he told MI that Beyer and other Germans suspected him of providing information. Still, Jaworski was not going to allow Petsch to make an issue out of Kunze's treason. Raising national security concerns, Jaworski would probably be able to keep out most of the information. He also counted on the MI people being careful enough that Petsch would not benefit from their testimony. Jaworski would do his part through strong evidentiary objections. One thing he had discovered early in the trial was Petsch's inability to cope with the objections. If Jaworski threw up enough static, Petsch either backed off or made mistakes that allowed the evidence to be stricken.

Second Lieutenant Robert G. Moreland, a young, tall, blond with a pencil-thin mustache, was to be Petsch's first witness. He served as the chief of the Security and Intelligence Division at the Tonkawa POW Camp. Jaworski had worked with him and told him to volunteer nothing unless Petsch hit it on the head.

"Do you recall," Petsch asked, "the time when Johannes Kunze, the war prisoner who was killed on or about the fourth day of November, 1943, came to Tonkawa Prisoner of War Camp?"

Moreland thought a moment. "I don't remember Kunze individually. Collectively, I do remember a group coming at that time."

"Shortly after the group of which Kunze was a part arrived, were you were advised—without stating what the advice was—by an American officer that prisoner of war Kunze was willing to talk to the American officers?"

Jaworski rose instantly from his chair. "Just a moment, if it please the court. That is hearsay of the rankest type, and we object to it on that ground. In addition to that, the matter is wholly immaterial and is incompetent, irrelevant, and extraneous, and not an issue in this case."

The law member nodded in agreement. "What is the purpose?"

"The purpose is simply to show that the witness

received the information; that following the receipt of that information, a contact was made."

Petsch was trying to obtain hearsay statements of people who weren't going to testify that Kunze was a spy working for the Americans. Asking for a summary of what they said didn't solve the problem. The law member sustained Jaworski's objection. Undeterred, Petsch tried another direction.

"Lieutenant, within the first thirty days after prisoner of war Kunze arrived at the Tonkawa Prisoner of War Camp, did any representative from the Department of Internal Security at Oklahoma City contact you for the purpose of interviewing prisoner of war Kunze?"

"Yes, I was contacted."

"Now, did you make the arrangements for the interview between prisoner of war Kunze and the representative of the Department of Internal Security of the United States Army from Oklahoma City?"

Lieutenant Moreland began to answer, but Jaworski shook his head no. "Just a moment," Jaworski said. "Unless it can be shown of this witness's own personal knowledge that an interview of that character took place, we object to it, because it would be hearsay as far as this witness is concerned."

"All right," Petsch said holding up his hands in surrender. "We'll withdraw the question." But once withdrawn, Petsch angled at it another way. "On or about the third day of September, 1943, do you know whether a representative from the Department of Internal Security of the United States Army, that section of the department located at Oklahoma

City—from the county intelligence section of that department—came to you and advised you that he desired an interview with prisoner of war Kunze?"

Moreland looked to Jaworski, then answered. "Yes, sir, he wanted an interview with that prisoner of war."

"Do you remember the name of that representative?"

"Just a minute," Jaworski said, throwing his legal pad on the table for show, "I don't think that would be material, and there are obvious reasons why the name ought not be mentioned. If counsel has any question about that, I would like to speak to him privately."

Several members of the jury were nodding in agreement. They did not seem pleased with the direction Petsch was taking his questions. No one, especially with the war still raging, wanted security compromised.

"All right," Petsch said, "we will waive that. I do have a final question. Who, if anyone, from your organization did you designate to make the arrangement for the interview?"

"Lieutenant Vickers B. Watts, not of my organization, and Technical Sergeant Bill Maddox."

Petsch turned to Jaworski and demanded that these witnesses be produced. Major Fuller motioned for the bailiff, but Jaworski stopped him and whispered, "Let me see if I can stop all this nonsense."

"As I understand it," Jaworski said, "—so there's no question about the matter—you are not in a position to testify of your own personal knowledge that *any* interview took place. That is correct, isn't it?"

"Yes, sir; that's true."

Jaworski turned to the jury. "The prosecution moves that this witness's entire testimony be stricken for the reason that it is immaterial and irrelevant, and nothing has been offered or introduced that is material to any issue in the case."

Petsch's face flushed bright red. "Counsel for the accused have not had two months to prepare this case, which the court is in a position to take knowledge of and already has knowledge of. Consequently, as far as this witness is concerned, counsel for the accused went up and talked to him, and we found that he was reluctant in his position to tell us anything."

Fifteen minutes later, after reproaches on both sides, the law member told Jaworski to bring the two witnesses. He would decide later whether to strike the testimony.

First Lieutenant Vickers B. Watts was a small, wiry man with a hard-scrabble Southern accent. He eyed Petsch with the wariness of a copperhead poised to strike.

"Lieutenant Watts, did you see prisoner of war Kunze at the Tonkawa Prisoner of War Camp just shortly after his arrival?"

"I saw him on the day of his arrival."

Pressing further, Petsch asked, "Just answer this question yes or no. Had you been directed to identify or find prisoner of war Kunze on the date of his arrival?"

Jaworski sat back with his fingers steepled. He had

spoken with Watts and given him some pointers on how to deal with Petsch.

"If the question is worded that way, I will have to answer it no."

"Were you directed to find or locate prisoner of war Kunze approximately or about the time of his arrival."

Watts frowned in concentration. "I will still have to answer that no."

"Well, were you asked by anybody to locate, or identify or find prisoner of war Kunze?" Petsch was having difficulty containing the frustration in his voice.

"No, sir, I was not."

Petsch shook his head. His voice was defeated. "Well, what happened—just tell the court what happened as to whether you did or did not locate prisoner of war Kunze on the date of his arrival."

"I can do that, sir." However, Watts sat stone-faced, waiting for Petsch to pry out every detail.

"Did you locate or find prisoner of war Kunze on the date of his arrival?"

"I did. The problem is they told us to look for a man named Kun. The only name close to that was Kunze."

"Did you see him, then?"

"I saw him, yes, sir."

"Now, was that as he came in and as his record was checked?"

"I saw him after he had been processed and as he was leaving the building in which the processing took place.

"All right," Petsch said, a glimmer of enthusiasm back in his voice. "Now, at that time did you place the prisoner of war Kunze and another group of prisoners in the charge of a sergeant for the purpose of having him taken to a barracks."

"I did."

"Did you receive the direction to locate and identify Kunze from your camp intelligence officer?"

"I was told by the camp intelligence officer."

Jaworski had no questions. Watts had yielded nothing for the defense. Petsch called his next witness, Sergeant Bill Maddox.

"Did you take charge of prisoner of war Johannes Kunze and take him to any particular place? Just say what you did when your attention was first directed to him," Petsch said.

Maddox, a large man with a bad overbite and thinning black hair, listened intently to Colonel Petsch's question. As with Lieutenant Watts, Jaworski had instructed him to only answer *exactly* what was asked.

Maddox said, "I was in charge of taking a detail of the prisoners from the compound where they were processed to their future barracks, and Lieutenant Watts called my attention to this particular man and told me to remember where I put him."

"Then did you carry out those instructions?"

"Yes, sir, I did."

"And you remember the barracks in which you placed him, is that correct?"

"Yes, sir. He was placed in the building by himself, alone."

"Then shortly after you placed this prisoner of war in a building by himself, did you see a man in civilian clothes, dressed in civilian clothes go into that same building."

After a long pause, Maddox said, "I did, sir."

"Do you know whether this man that you saw dressed in civilian clothes entered the building where Johannes Kunze . . . where you had left Johannes Kunze?"

"Yes, sir."

"Approximately how long did he . . . if you know, approximately how long did he remain in the building with Johannes Kunze?"

Maddox looked toward the ceiling for a moment. "Approximately thirty minutes."

Petsch never failed to amaze Jaworski. When the information was minor, Petsch could be an effective questioner. Fortunately, on the larger matters he continued to bungle along. Petsch had made some effective points with this witness, and Jaworski intended to downplay its significance.

"Johannes Kunze was taken in that building to work, was he not?" Jaworski asked.

"Yes, sir."

"And, as a matter of fact, a number of prisoners were taken to different buildings to sweep up, clean up, weren't they?"

"They were, sir."

"And he was placed in this particular building to do that work, was he not?"

"The same identical detail."

Critically Jaworski stated, "You don't keep up with

the work in the operations of your intelligence officer at that camp, do you? It is not a part of your function to keep up with that is it?"

"No, sir."

"And you don't know what prisoners he interviews or what prisoners he doesn't interview, do you?"

Maddox looked a bit hurt at Jaworski's tone. It couldn't be helped.

"No, sir."

"And you don't know what his system is—by that I mean whether he might take fifteen or twenty prisoners and interview them at random or whether he selects certain ones to interview. You don't know that, either, do you?"

Maddox looked a bit annoyed. "No, sir, I don't."

Jaworski did not wait until Maddox had even stepped down before he was making his motion.

"The prosecution moves that the entire testimony of this witness be stricken from the record as well as the testimony of Lieutenant Moreland which had been given subject to being connected up, and for the further reason that this testimony is wholly irrelevant and immaterial—it proves nothing."

Petsch pulled himself wearily from his chair, but his voice was spirited. "We want to say that this is some of the most material testimony that we have in this case. In the event that this court finds the defendants, any of the accused, guilty of murder, then the next big question that has to be considered by the court will be the amount of punishment which should be awarded. . . ."

Punishment. Jaworski smiled to himself. Petsch was giving away any hope of an acquittal.

"For the purpose of determining that fact, there is no factor to come before the court which would require more serious consideration and bear greater weight as the resolution of the question of whether or not this man was a traitor to his country."

The law member stopped Petsch. "Let me ask you a question here. Are you submitting this testimony merely for the consideration of the court relative to clemency?"

"Whatever the court may deem it useful for," Petsch said spreading his arms expansively, "and whatever light it may throw upon these transactions. Let's not be technical about the matter . . . We are not trying a soldier of the United States Army here."

The law member listened to the argument for ten minutes, then once again put off his ruling.

It doesn't matter, thought Jaworski. Petsch had as good as put the noose around his clients' necks; he was talking about clemency before he had rested the defense case.

14

Brothers in Arms

Camp Gruber, Oklahoma
January 20, 1944

COLONEL JAWORSKI HAD BEEN GIVEN A LONG LIST OF
German POWs who planned to testify on behalf of
First Sergeant Beyer. All were noncommissioned officers; all were combat veterans of North Africa.
Jaworski suspected they would do everything possible
to protect a brother in arms and know miraculously
little about a murder that had taken place in their
presence. Sergeant Erwin Brandt gave the first of the
almost identical testimony from these men.

Petsch asked, "Did you attend a meeting in the
mess hall of Company Four in the prisoner of war
camp on the night of November 4, 1943?"

"Yes."

"Were you asked to attend that meeting?"

Brandt, a bulky man with a large jaw and dark
features, snapped back a quick answer as if in formation. "No. I heard that the company was to go to the
mess hall. I was in the washroom, and then I went
likewise to the mess hall."

Brandt described how once all two hundred members of the company were present, First Sergeant Beyer held the spy paper up for inspection and asked for Kunze's comment.

"After the paper was read, did you see Johannes Kunze at the meeting?"

"Yes."

"Where was Johannes Kunze at the time you first saw him, and what was he doing?"

"He stood up front near First Sergeant Beyer, and he was asked whether he had written that letter. . . . But he didn't answer. . . . Shouts came from the mass to the effect of whether or not he had written it. . . . He didn't answer anything. . . . Then shouts became loud to the effect that the man is all white and he was perspiring on his forehead, and then shouts became audible to the effect, 'Give him a beating so he won't do it again,' or approximately something along those words."

"And then what happened, if anything."

Brandt took a deep breath. "Then there were shouts throughout the room, and people began to crowd Sergeant Beyer away from Kunze, and blows fell, and there was general tumult."

Petsch's voice was serious, prodding, "Before, or at any time while you were in a position to see Johannes Kunze, did you ever see Sergeant Beyer strike a blow against or onto Johannes Kunze?"

"No," he said confidently. "He didn't hit him."

"When the fight first started, or at any other time while the fight was going on, or the tumult was going on, did you observe anybody trying to stop the fight?"

"Yes," Brandt said. "First Sergeant Beyer," he said, pointing to Beyer.

"State what, if anything, First Sergeant Beyer did to stop the fight."

Brandt nodded his head. "When Beyer had been crowded away and when he saw that a beating was about to take place, he said, 'For God's sake, children, don't beat him, or otherwise we will get in trouble with the Americans,' or words to that effect." Then Brandt added, "He said so several times."

"Was the statement made in an ordinary tone of voice or was it made by First Sergeant Beyer in a loud tone of voice?"

"He said it very loudly."

"Thank you."

Jaworski rose from his seat slowly and fired his first question. "Since you came to the camp at Tonkawa, the accused Beyer has been your leader?"

"Yes," Brandt answered proudly.

Then, quickly changing course, Jaworski asked, "Did you see anyone strike Kunze?"

"No."

"Was he beaten at all in the mess hall that evening?" Jaworski shrugged in disbelief.

"Yes," Brandt said, looking straight ahead passively.

"How long were you in the mess hall while Kunze was being beaten?"

"I cannot tell the time exactly. When the tumult started, I got up from my seat and went out over the tables, and that may have taken me four or five minutes, and during that time—"

"Why did you leave?"

"I was sick and had pains, and I wanted to go back to bed."

Jaworski's voice dripped with sarcasm. "Did the sight of Kunze being beaten make you sick?"

Brandt frowned once he understood the translation. "No," he said, locking eyes with Jaworski. "I was sick before that."

"About how many different persons were striking Kunze during the several minutes you were in the mess hall?"

Jaworski waited for the answer, his arms crossed over his chest, his face set in displeasure. He might not be able to force the truth out of these Germans, but he certainly was going to let the jury know what he thought of them.

"Well," Brandt said, "that's hard to say because people were standing around Kunze, and from the distance one could see only arms and some feet, and I can't say anything about it."

"Would you say that there were as many as twenty prisoners of war whom you saw beat Kunze?"

"I can't say anything about the number. I didn't see anything concerning it, and people were surrounding Kunze and I can't name any numbers . . . I can only say that there was a beating. I cannot give any number since I had to pay attention to my route, since I had to clamber over tables to get out."

Jaworski shook his head. "No more questions for this witness."

The last of eight German witnesses to describe Beyer's attempt to stop the beating was Gerhard

Grummel, a twenty-four-year-old blond sergeant who looked to be in his teens. He had the intense stare of a young man who had seen more than his share of combat.

Petsch took Grummel through his combat service in Africa, then turned to more direct questioning. "During the lifetime of Johannes Kunze, did you know him?"

Grummel crossed his legs; he seemed completely at ease. "I've known him since Tonkawa. We were rather friendly."

"Are you a close friend of any of the accused?"

"No."

His lack of bias established, Petsch set the scene of Beyer's reading of the spy note and Kunze's failure to respond to the accusations.

"Do you know what happened when Kunze didn't make a statement, after he finished looking at the paper?"

Grummel said matter-of-factly, "There was a general congestion, and he received a few slaps in the face."

A few slaps. The description made Jaworski want to throttle this young Nazi.

"Before or immediately after the fight started, did you see First Sergeant Beyer?"

"Yes, he was about six meters away."

"After the fight started, did anybody try to restore order—attempt to stop the fight or restore order."

Petsch held up his finger, indicating to answer the simple question first.

"Yes."

"What did they do?"

"First Sergeant Beyer shouted several times that we should not hit, we would get in trouble with the Americans. . . . He was shouting at the men to stop beating Kunze, but the tumult was too great."

Grummel claimed to have wandered outside at this point and that he had seen Kunze exit the mess hall.

"Did you at any time while you remained between the mess halls see Johannes Kunze leave the mess hall?"

"Yes."

"What door did he come out of when you saw him leave?"

Grummel thought a moment, seeming to orient his directions. "Out of the east door."

"Did he walk out or run out or was he carried out by other prisoners of war?"

"He came walking out . . . , and he stumbled over a post, a low fence. There is a fence in front of the door so that one should not walk over the flower beds."

"When Kunze fell over this low fence, do you know what, if anything, happened to him?"

"I don't know," Grummel said innocently.

"Did you see anybody or any number of men grab hold of Kunze after he got out into the dark?"

"No."

"Your witness," Petsch said.

This was their damn *Heilige Geist,* thought Jaworski. A man was murdered, beaten to death with a milk bottle, fists and feet, yet no human, at least no German POW, had anything to do with it. They were no better than the Klan lynchings he had heard about as a boy. Hiding behind sheets, none of them with the courage to act in broad daylight.

Jaworski's voice was harsh as he began his questioning. "Is it your testimony that you saw Kunze receive only a few slaps that evening?"

"And a few kicks in the behind," Grummel said, grinning slightly.

"And you believe Johannes died from a few slaps in his face and a few kicks on his behind—that is your testimony?" Jaworski glared incredulously at Grummel.

"I can't say that."

"When Kunze came out of that door, you say he walked?"

"Yes."

"Was he so badly crippled at that time that he could not run?"

"No," Grummel said slowly. "His pants were about to slip down."

Jaworski decided to slow the pace of his questions. Grummel knew more than his clipped answers to Petsch let on.

"Well, was the fact that his pants had slipped the reason that he couldn't run fast as he came through the door?"

"Yes."

"Before Kunze ran out of the door, he had run into the kitchen to try to escape from the others, hadn't he?"

"Yes," Grummel said testily.

"And he ran into the storeroom?"

"Yes."

"And he tried to get out of the back door, out of the storeroom, didn't he?"

Seeming bored, Grummel answered, "Yes."

"And you were running behind Kunze that entire time, weren't you?"

Grummel shook his head adamantly. "No, I was in the back of the mess hall."

Jaworski walked back to the prosecution table and retrieved the diagram of the mess hall. "Then, how do you know that he tried to get out of the back door in the storeroom? There is a wall between the kitchen and storeroom, isn't there?" Jaworski held the map in front of Grummel.

Grummel pursed his lips. "No, there is a door in between."

Jaworski tapped his finger on the map. "There's a small door on the side over here, and that is all the opening there is?"

"Yes."

Stay focused, Jaworski told himself. Just make sure you convict the ones who have been caught. He took the map of the mess hall back to the prosecution table and exchanged it for the pictures of Kunze's savaged body.

"Was Kunze bleeding when he left the mess hall?"

"His nose was bleeding some."

Scowling for the jury, Jaworski asked, "He had only a few scratches in the face and a bloody nose; that was all, was it?"

"Yes," Grummel said flatly.

"Do you recognize this picture?" Jaworski thrust the picture of Kunze's battered body at Grummel.

"Do you?"

Grummel glanced at the photo and attempted to hand it back, but Jaworski had purposefully stepped back.

"No."

"Did you ever see anyone look like this?"

"No."

"Does that look to you like only a few *scratches and a bloody nose?*"

"No."

"Do you tell this court now, under oath, that Johannes Kunze did not look like this when you saw him outside the mess hall on that night?"

Grummel stared straight ahead. Jaworski could picture the Germans chasing Kunze around the mess hall like a pack of jackals, tearing at him until they had weakened him for the kill. Yet Grummel sat cool as could be claiming to have been "friends" with Kunze.

"Yes, Kunze did not look like this."

"When you were standing outside, watching Kunze, who were you talking to?"

He thought a moment. "Kessler. A man from another platoon."

"And what did you and Kessler talk about?"

"This case, that this was a great act of cowardice."

"That the striking of Kunze by these men was an act of cowardice?"

Grummel looked at Jaworski as if he were completely out of his mind. "No, the treason to the fatherland."

"And that's all you were talking about?" Jaworski

mirrored Grummel's look. "You had no discussion about the condition of the man Kunze, who was lying there on the ground dying?"

"No," Grummel said, dismissing Jaworski's tone with a shrug.

We were friends. "No more questions," Jaworski said.

15

The Accused

FOR WEEKS BEYER HAD BEEN WAITING TO EXPLAIN TO THE Americans why he had been forced to tell his men about Kunze's treachery. Now eleven officers sat in judgment. Petsch had told him they were all combat arms officers, men who understood the need for iron discipline. They, of all people, should understand that a soldier could not permit a traitor to go unpunished, lest they be punished by their superiors.

Petsch questioned Beyer about his eight years of military service, then why he suspected Kunze. Beyer related how he had received the spy note and had searched the mail for writing that matched that of the note. Now it was time to tell the Americans his thought process, why he was compelled to let his men judge Kunze.

Beyer began in forceful, clipped German: "I sat down at the back of my room. Not very many people came in. There was another sergeant in there besides me. I read the note again and compared the two

177

instruments again, and then I came to the conclusion that I couldn't just let this thing go. . . . I had to do something to prevent this man from getting any further information from his comrades. . . . I compared those two documents, and I came to the conclusion that in order to protect myself I had to read this to the company, this document, in order to prevent that when I go back to Germany I am put before a court-martial as an accessory to treason."

"Did you at any time during that day call a meeting of any of the other noncommissioned officers in your company?"

"No, not according to my recollection."

"Did you call a meeting for that night?"

"Yes . . . the men assembled, and I asked for silence and read this note." Beyer pointed to the spy note that Petsch handed to him. "Then I stepped off to the right and asked the company, that is all the members of the company, to come up and look at the letter and a sample of Kunze's handwriting, and I placed them both on the top of a table. I bent or folded Kunze's letter in such a way that nobody could see who had written it. And then people came up and looked at it and in consequence, of course, I had to step back a bit."

"Did Johannes Kunze come up and look at the two documents?"

"Yes," Beyer said with no hesitation, "he came up front. . . . He didn't say anything but his eyes were wide open, and he was pale and had beads of perspiration on the forehead. . . . After that Kunze didn't say anything, and people standing around him noticed by his looks and by his silence that he was feeling guilty. There arose a tumult and a lot of noise. I only know that the ring around him became larger and larger, and I was partly shoved and partly walked toward the entrance. . . . Due to the fact that there were about three tables missing, there was a lot of empty space there, and in this space there developed a fight, a fist fight, a beating; and then I saw many hands beating, and it may be possible that perhaps I saw Sergeant Seidel beating there, but I am not sure of it. I can't say that for sure anymore."

"Then what did you do, if anything?"

"Strangely," Beyer said with a sigh, "my thoughts at that time were in Germany. I imagined how at that time, perhaps at that very moment, American or English bombers dropped bombs over Hamburg and by doing so perhaps soon will destroy my family."

Beyer looked to the jury, but they showed no emotion. If only they could know the horrible dreams he had of losing his Edgar, of finally finding him under the pile of rubble only to have him disappear.

Petsch went right back to the night of the beating. "Do you know whether anybody made any effort, did anyone attempt to stop the fight or to protect Kunze?"

"Yes. While I was moving toward the door, I turned around maybe two or three times and demanded that they should stop with this beating because I foresaw that this would bring about complications. However, the idea that they might kill Kunze did not enter my mind."

"Did you at any time leave the mess hall during the time that the fighting was going on?"

"Yes, I went outside, but where I went or what I did out there I can't remember and didn't mention that in my previous statements because of the fact I couldn't recollect it exactly. . . . I believe I went to the orderly room and my room."

"Did you come back to the mess hall?"

"Yes."

"Was the fight still continuing?"

"Yes, the brawl was going on about the same place."

"After you reentered the mess hall the second time, did you attempt to do anything to stop the fight?"

Beyer sat up straighter, head raised. "Yes, I went to that one table right near the east door of the mess hall, I stepped onto the bench which is fastened to the table, and shouted in a loud voice, 'stop it, stop' but whether or not I added anything to that I can't say right now."

Petsch extended his hand to Jaworski, indicating that he was finished.

Experienced defense lawyers know it is always dangerous putting a defendant on the stand. In Beyer's case, it was just plain foolish to put the defendant on the stand unless he could deny being at the scene or had a true self-defense claim in a murder case. Jaworski planned to hang the defendants with their own words and deeds.

Jaworski said, "Sergeant, did you consider the note in question to be traitorous?" His voice was even, no hint this was laying a trap.

"Yes."

"Were you outraged when you read its contents?" Jaworski pursed his lips, trying to indicate this would have been the only reasonable response under the circumstances.

Beyer sat ramrod straight, his answer barked in a command voice. "Yes."

Kindly, like a concerned father, Jaworski asked, "Did you believe that any good German soldier would be outraged upon reading its contents?"

"I was convinced of that."

You're laying a snare, thought Jaworski, wait until he's fully inside the loop before you yank it shut.

"Then, you expected when your soldiers would be advised of the contents of this note that they would be greatly outraged?"

Beyer frowned. Damn, thought Jaworski, this was the problem with having translation. It gives him too long a time to formulate an evasion.

"That is hard to say." Beyer shifted in his chair. "I myself was cut to the quick that such a man should betray those things for which we stood at the front for four years already."

Try from another angle, Jaworski told himself. "And you expected the majority of your soldiers to react the same way at the meeting, didn't you?"

"Yes."

Good. He's inside the snare.

"Didn't you expect that two hundred outraged soldiers would bring disorder?"

A crease of worry passed over Beyer's face. Yet his voice was gruff, guttural. "I did not expect that he would be beaten in such a manner. It had never occurred to me that he would be beaten in such a manner that he would die."

Quickly Jaworski added, "But when you called the meeting, you did expect the group to administer a beating?"

"I knew that there was the possibility that he might be beaten, yes."

"Knowing that there was such a possibility, you took no measures for any of your sergeants or other noncommissioned officers to be stationed throughout the meeting to preserve order and guard against such a beating."

Slowly, Beyer was lowering his guard. Jaworski knew it was just a matter of framing the questions right to tap into his feeling of betrayal.

"No, I was too excited to get an overall picture of the entire affair. I was internally much too moved and much too insulted by the very thought that there should be such a man who could betray his fatherland in such a manner . . ."

Then circling back to this area several questions later, Jaworski asked, "Why didn't you call the American guards when you were on the outside during those two or three minutes you left the mess hall?"

"First, I wasn't even thinking about that; second, I, to some extent, thought Kunze deserved a licking."

Jaworski tried not to hurry.

"Then, the matter of giving Kunze a licking had your blessing?"

"Yes, I thought that was all right."

Jaworski had to contain his smile. Though he suspected Beyer didn't know it, he had just put the noose around his own neck. He had known the "licking" was a possibility and had given it his blessing. The law was clear on this point, whether Petsch appreciated the finer points or not. Beyer was an aider and abettor to the murder. He had set the riot in motion, had given the "licking" his okay. That the beating developed into something worse than he had anticipated was not a defense. Jaworski had two areas left that he wanted to damage the first sergeant with— his hate of Kunze and his lack of truthfulness about who was involved in the beating.

"When you came back into the mess hall, did you step in front of Kunze and offer him any protection?"

"No."

"Before this note that you consider traitorous was delivered to you, you had already felt unkindly toward Kunze?"

Beyer eyed Jaworski suspiciously, then answered, "No, not before I got the note."

Jaworski raised his eyebrows for the juror's sake. "Didn't you complain about Kunze not obeying your orders even before November 2, 1943?"

"Yes, I did say that."

Jaworski started firing questions at Beyer, knowing they would all show that he had been less than truthful.

"And you ordered Kunze to do something once, and he told you that you weren't in Germany now, isn't that correct?"

Beyer looked surprised, as if he couldn't believe the Americans knew this. "Yes, he gave me an answer approximately to that effect; Kunze said to me, 'Well, that time is past,' or something like that."

"And Kunze also said he expected to stay in America and bring his family here after the war, didn't he?"

More casually, "Yes, I heard that once from a member of his barracks, and I don't recall who that was."

"And by reason of those remarks you had referred to Kunze as a 'bum' person, hadn't you?"

Beyer drew in his chin. "I never called him a 'bum.'"

"Well, you didn't exactly like him on that account?"

"No, and that explains itself."

Beyer had regained his stony composure. It was time to see whether he would still protect his fellow Germans.

"Were the lights on the entire time that you were in the mess hall?"

Beyer began to hesitate with each answer. Apparently, he was beginning to figure out that he was hurting himself. "The light was on in the mess room, and it was not on in the kitchen."

Jaworski walked up to the witness stand and looked Beyer directly in the eyes. "Are you willing to tell this court who the men were who were beating Kunze in the mess hall that night?"

Beyer would not look him in the face. "I can't tell you that because there were too many."

Pointing toward the jury, Jaworski said, "Tell the court as many as you remember."

Seemingly unfazed, Beyer answered while staring past Jaworski. "I can't tell the court exactly who that was. I didn't see things clearly enough to say to anyone, 'Well, you did it.' I could not point out anybody and say, 'You did it.'"

Jaworski started to walk back to his seat, then turned and asked a final series of questions. His tone was casual again, even though the answers to his questions about who controlled the compounds at night was essential to proving Beyer's responsibility in Kunze's death.

"Was one of the orders you received from the Americans for you to keep peace in your company?"

Beyer contemplated the question a long time and said: "We prisoners of war were never notified concerning any rights or duties. We were never told what we were allowed to do or what we had to do."

"No more questions," he said.

Jaworski finally let himself smile. Beyer had made the mistake of being too accurate about some details, then not remembering the most damaging part of the night. And unbeknownst to Beyer, Jaworski had the former camp commander standing by to contradict Beyer's supposed lack of authority.

Beyer stood to return to his seat at the counsel table when Jaworski suddenly motioned for him to remain seated. The president of the panel, Colonel Desobry, had some questions.

"First Sergeant," Desobry said, reading a question

from his legal pad, "upon your second visit to the mess hall, you attempted to quell this disorder by word of mouth and failed, that's so, isn't it?"

"Yes, I tried and I failed."

"If this situation was out of hand, why didn't you call the American military authorities to put down this disorder?"

"I don't know what influenced me in that way," Beyer said.

Jaworski watched the old colonel check the questions off his list, seeming to satisfy himself that there was no mitigation in this case. Desobry indicated with his finger he had one final area of inquiry.

"If you did not think Kunze might be killed, then, why did you hold the meeting so late at night when there were no American authorities in the compound?"

Several other officers nodded that this was on their minds as well.

Beyer thought a long time, then said, "I don't know."

Desobry shook his head in apparent anger as Beyer left the stand. There was no sympathy for him. He was an NCO who had allowed one of his men to be killed. He had set the arena for a bloodbath, then stepped aside and claimed that he should not be held accountable. Whether Beyer, or Petsch for that matter, realized it, Beyer was going to pay.

After lunch Jaworski recalled his final witness, Major Polsley, the former commandant of the camp at Tonkawa. The heavyset Texan retook the stand, the walk to the stand seeming to wind him.

"Major Polsley, I wish you would explain to the court what system was followed at the Tonkawa Prisoner of War Camp with respect to the maintaining of order and discipline in the compounds of the camp after count had been made?"

Polsley settled into the chair like he was having his afternoon coffee break and had a good one to tell the boys.

"At both the morning and evening count, as soon as the count was made, the American officers and noncommissioned officers, would go back to their companies or to the officers' mess for their meals. The count was twice a day, once before eight in the morning and then approximately five forty-five in the evening. At night the jurisdiction or authority was in the hands of German noncommissioned officers."

Petsch rose angrily. "We object to that statement, 'the jurisdiction or authority was in the hands of German noncommissioned officers,' because that is just his conclusion . . ."

Excellent, thought Jaworski, draw their attention to the matter. He'd rephrase and emphasize it even more.

"I think you could put it differently," the law member said.

Jaworski nodded deferentially.

"To whom did you, as commanding officer of the prisoner of war camp, leave the matter of order and discipline in the compound after the American personnel had retired?"

"I'll answer it this way," Polsley said, drawling hard on *this*. "The authority was given to the American commissioned officers to pick the first or ranking sergeant of the German company."

"Thank you, Major," Jaworski said.

It was now clear that Beyer was in charge that night. Every man in a company would not have shown up at the mess hall at ten at night unless they were ordered. Petsch could claim all day that Beyer had no authority, but his bearing and strict demeanor told the jurors otherwise.

After the commandant left, Jaworski turned to the defense table. "One final matter. We have a handwriting expert here from Washington, D.C., who can testify as to whether the Hamburg paper and the letter to Kunze's wife were, in fact, written by the same person. The prosecution does not plan to call this witness because the government views the question of authorship as immaterial. In fairness to the court and the defense, however, the witness is available." Jaworski knew the witness would testify that the documents were both written by the same person.

To Jaworski's surprise, Petsch did not want to call the witness. "If the court pleases, on the part of the accused we want to say that we do not have time enough to worry about any witnesses on immaterial matters. We would like the record to show that."

Immaterial. If the defense theory of the case was that Kunze was a traitor who deserved to be killed, wasn't proof that he authored the note necessary? How could the defense walk away from this opportunity to highlight their theory? At times Jaworski almost felt like laughing at Petsch's bumbling theatrics.

"Very well," Jaworski said, "the prosecution rests."

Petsch moved again that the spy handlers' testimony be admitted. It no longer mattered. Jaworski didn't object, and the testimony was admitted.

16

Closing Arguments

Camp Gruber, Oklahoma
January 25, 1944

JAWORSKI STOOD DIRECTLY IN FRONT OF THE JURY READY
to give his summation. He knew there were weak
areas where a good defense lawyer might make in-
roads. If he had been the defense counsel, he would
have argued that this was a case of voluntary man-
slaughter; that a killing had occurred in the sudden
heat of passion, but that it was not murder. Fortunately, Petsch had made the mistake of trying for
every defense possible, even when they were contra-
dictory. Jaworski planned to keep his argument on an
emotional level in hopes the jury would make an all-
or-nothing decision.

"May it please the court," Jaworski said, bowing
slightly to the law officer, "for several days we have
witnessed a trial most unique in American history; we
have seen the protecting arms of a great democracy
reach out to give strength, fairness, and justice to men
who belong to the enemy; we have seen that no matter

who the accused may be, when he comes before an American tribunal his every right is safeguarded."

There will be no Nazi propaganda out of this trial.

"But let us not forget, no, let us not forget, that Johannes Kunze was also entitled to that same protection—the protection accorded by that flag," Jaworski said, pointing to the American flag in the corner of the room. "He, too, was a German prisoner of war detained by this power, and as such was entitled to all of the protection that this power accords to prisoners of war. What sort of trial was Johannes Kunze given? These men say Kunze did wrong." Jaworski pointed accusingly at the five defendants. "Well, this court doesn't know whether he did wrong. I don't know whether he did wrong, but let's assume for the sake of argument for just a moment that he did do wrong. What chance was he given, what sort of a trial was Johannes Kunze given? In a space of a few minutes, these men who are sitting here served as accusers, as witnesses, as prosecutors, as judge, as jury, and as executioners. That is the sort of a trial Johannes Kunze was given. How can that possibly be justified? What chance was Johannes Kunze given to defend himself? Oh, they said that he was asked whether or not he signed this note and that he said nothing. I don't believe that ever took place, and later I am going to point out to the court why the record speaks undeniably that it didn't take place. But let us assume that such actions took place. Johannes Kunze was entitled—assuming for the sake of argument that he wrote that note—to show the facts and circumstances surrounding the writing of that note. No one knows why or how the note came to be. If Johannes Kunze wrote it, he is the only person that could have told this court, or any other court, that he wrote it. What were the facts; what were the circumstances? He was never given an opportunity to say that."

All along Jaworski had worried about the mitigation that Kunze's spying might provide. He planned to deflect it with illusions of mob violence and oblique references to Nazi death camps.

Jaworski continued: "It all goes to show what happens when a mob sets out to take a man's life and does not let the courts, which are properly appointed for such purposes, judge the wrong of that man. Well, actually in law, it is wholly immaterial whether he wrote the note or not. You cannot take a man, I care not whether he be murderer or rapist, and throw him into the hands of a mob and let them execute him simply because he was guilty; and it is no defense that the victim was a murderer or rapist when the men who are guilty of taking his life are brought to trial. It has to be that way. There is no difference between a man being killed in cold blood by one person or being killed in cold blood as the result of a surging throng or mob. The authorities, the American law of jurisprudence has so said many, many times. It is not a part of the law of this land that just because a man is unworthy he may be killed—killed without trial, killed in cold blood. Now, that sort of a thing may be termed *liquidation* in some places"—Jaworski tossed a glance to the defendants—"but in America there is only one name for it, and that is *murder*."

Nazis, death camps. America was still fighting Hitler's Germany, and Jaworski planned to use that evil to help convict all five men. What these men did was just a different kind of liquidation of an undesirable.

With the emotional tone set, Jaworski was ready to explain the law. "On the murder count, you are interested in two things. First, was this a case of malice aforethought, and what has the law said that constitutes malice aforethought; secondly, what is the situation when an event occurs during which a man is struck by not only one or two men insofar as the fatal blows are concerned but that a number of men participated in the events leading up to his death."

Jaworski began the slow task of explaining how the defendants' actions amounted to murder. After citing numerous treatises, he explained why these facts demonstrated malice. "In other words, all you need is an intention to do an unlawful act, and if it results in the death of a person, it is murder. What does that mean as applied to the facts in this case? Is there any doubt in the mind of any member of this court that the meeting held that evening was called for the purpose of doing an unlawful act—that is, an assault on Kunze? It is an unlawful act. During a gathering held for an unlawful purpose to do an unlawful act, actions were taken that resulted in the death of Kunze. If the consequences are such as to bring about the death of a person, it constitutes murder, and everyone present who participated, or aided or abetted in the act, is guilty of murder."

That was the general rule, but Jaworski wanted to make sure they understood why Beyer was responsible. He picked up a law book and read: " 'When one is present encouraging, assisting, and advising another to do an unlawful act, the law presumes that the one acting is induced to commit the act by the presence and encouragement of the other.' All right, Beyer's very presence, no matter how much he might have denied exactly what he had in mind at the beginning in the session he held that afternoon before the meeting, his very presence lent the greatest encouragement to the commission of that act. Here is a man who is the leader of the group that stands before the company and who—according to the sworn statements solemnly given by these other accused in their reports written back in their cells, written when they had in mind wanting to help themselves as much as they possibly could, written in their own handwriting, as some of the witnesses here testified—said, 'There is a traitor in this group.' Why, what chance did any man have after that? Here is the leader saying, 'There is a traitor in this group.' Now, can you expect a group of men when a thing is presented to them in that light to turn a cold shoulder to the statement of their leader? Of course not. . . . Obviously, the fact that a defendant regrets that the killing occurred in no way lessens his responsibility."

Several of the jurors seemed puzzled. Jaworski knew that aider and abettor law was difficult to follow, but he planned to tell a story. "Why, that has got to be the law. If that wasn't the law, how could you ever hold responsible those who engage in mob violence? Every man is the one who pulls the rope. It will be one fellow that buys, another gets the gasoline and furnishes the automobile, there will be a few more that storm the place to take the man, there will be more who whip up the frenzy of the crowd, and usually the man who makes the big speech and who is the leader." He turned and stared at Beyer a long time. "The leader seldom takes part in the actual striking of the blows or the pulling of the rope. He whips up the frenzy, the fury, and then there will be just a few that actually pull the rope. It doesn't make any difference what particular participation they had in the matter; the result was that a man died, that a man was killed—murdered—and anyone who took part in that proceeding is liable as a principle under the authorities."

The puzzled looks disappeared. It was time to attack the traitor issue.

"Well, things have been said about the bad character of Johannes Kunze. I don't know whether he had a bad character or not. Insofar as the law is concerned, it is immaterial. They referred to him as a traitor, and I know that we can expect the opposition to give a great speech on treason. I want to say this: It would be a fine state of affairs if prisoners of war were licensed to kill one of their number every time he was interviewed by an intelligence officer. Just assume that Kunze was interviewed by an intelligence officer, the record fails to bear out an actual interview, but just assume it. Why, men with reason know there are literally hundreds of men interviewed who never furnish one bit of information. Are suspicious persons, are persons wicked of mind and heart, are persons who engage in venting a malicious feeling, to be licensed to commit murder just because a man has been interviewed by an intelligence officer?" He shrugged for effect.

Jaworski made a small digression about the law of riot, how one could originally assemble for peaceful purposes, then form the intent for unlawful purposes. But he could not help returning to the traitor issue.

"Talk about a traitor," he shook his head in dismay. "What about the cowardice of dozens of men who lunge upon one man who is helpless to defend himself? Talk about a traitor. What about the gangsterism, the mobism of a number of men who are swooping down upon one helpless, defenseless person? I can't see a lot of difference. That is the sort of a situation that their own letters, their own reports, tell. Bloody and bleeding, badly wounded, that man tries every way on earth to seek escape. He is hounded and pursued and beaten, cups were thrown at him, everything on earth done that comprises cruelty and barbarity. Well, we can't get all the men that were guilty." Jaworski held his hands, palms up. "You never do when you have a mob. But we have a number of them, and it isn't our fault; it isn't the government's fault that more were not apprehended. I want to pause to pay tribute to the men who investigated this case and who were able to bring before this court the facts that were brought here. They did a marvelous job, and they deserve a tremendous amount of credit. It isn't their fault that there are only five accused standing before this court instead of ten or fifteen or more. But it is not to be considered by this court in its deliberations. The fact remains that those who are not here are equally guilty with the others, and it is no defense, no justification, no extenuation to say, 'Well, you haven't got all of them.' "

Jaworski stopped and took a drink of water. He wanted a pause for all his information to sink in. He decided to hit Beyer's culpability one more time.

"There is much to be said about the accused Beyer not having interfered, not having made any effort to stop that meeting. You and I know, as a matter of fact, that he had ample opportunity. The statements he made in cross-examination, I know, are deeply impressed on your minds. They couldn't help but be, because they brought out so very cogently what opportunities this man had to avoid this murder if he had been the least bit interested in doing so. Why did he call the meeting so late at night? As a member of this court so aptly brought out in one of his questions, there was no reason for that late hour. If it was just for the purpose of advising the multitude that there was someone in their midst who should be shunned or such as that, why not do it in the morning while the American guards were present, or why not do it at some other hour? Then, in addition to that, he said he was outside for about three minutes. That strange, strange interlude." Jaworski huffed for emphasis. "He hasn't told us what he did during those three minutes.

There comes to his vision the thought that probably he went over to the orderly room, but he can't remember what he did in those two or three minutes. One thing he didn't do, that he could have done if he had been the least bit interested in sparing that man's life, was to send out a call for help."

He took a deep breath, ready for his conclusion.

"I say to this court what has happened here, what has taken place, is either murder or it isn't anything. It is not a function of the trial judge advocate . . . to say to this court what sentence should be imposed on any accused. That is a function that this court and this court alone, without suggestion from anyone, imposes. But it is the duty of the trial judge advocate to tell this court what offense in his opinion has been committed, and I say to you, to the best of my ability, based on a study of the authorities, and the facts in this case as applied to those authorities, that the offense of murder has been here committed. It is either murder or it isn't anything.

"An American soldier who would be found guilty of murder by mob, by taking the life of a man by mob, under the circumstances here present, would be found guilty of murder by an American court-martial. It is just as much murder if it is committed by someone else who is under the jurisdiction of American law. There is no reason why an exception should be made in this case.

"I just want to say to this court that they are pleading, will probably plead, for sympathy. When that is considered by this court, I want this court, as I know it will, in fairness to the entire facts in this case, to consider the sympathy that was extended by these accused to Johannes Kunze on the night in question. What sympathy was extended by these accused on the wife and three children of the deceased living in Germany. They didn't extend Johannes Kunze any sympathy, and they are not in a position to ask for any sympathy. It is an act that they committed; it is their responsibility. They can ask for no more than a fair application of the laws of this land for the commission of those offenses.

"I thank this court."

Petsch rose slowly from his chair to address the jury, then stood poised, one hand in his pocket—a casual scarecrow.

"I want to say to you gentlemen that at this time my inferiority complex has been multiplied, and I come before you representing these accused more handicapped now in the presentation of the facts upon which we are relying. We of the defense are relying for a judgment entirely different from that which the trial judge advocate states was his conclusion and should come from this court. On the side of the government there are two extraordinary lawyers of ability, with practically unlimited time for study and investigation on their hands because the enterprise in which they are engaged is the one very purpose for which they are in the service. On the other hand, counsel for the accused in trials before general courts-martial are in this case and performing the duties asked for them as counsel for the accused, and it is only incidental to their army vocations."

Petsch's disclaimer about being an infantry officer

worried Jaworski. It was the sort of remark that would cause the Germans to call foul play. He had told headquarters that they should put the very best possible defense lawyer on this case, that the facts were clear enough that it wouldn't matter. But he had lost in that argument.

Following his apology for the defense's ability, Petsch took several minutes arguing that the riot charge was not valid because there had been no value established for the property. Jaworski was pleased. Worrying about whether the broken crockery had value would not acquit five men accused of murder. Then, just as suddenly, Petsch veered off into what seemed like mitigation of the offense.

"When we come to the matter of considering the serious portion of this offense, what do we start with? We start with determining whether or not there are any circumstances in this case which excuse or justify the killing to begin with. Whenever an accused, or a group of accused, are tried for murder, without any exception, when a man reads a headline in the paper that says such and such a murder was committed, or when the word 'murder' is mentioned the first time to a human being, the first question in his mind is 'What kind of a man was the deceased; what did he do?' That is the natural question to be asked because it is unnatural for human beings to kill each other. It just isn't reasonable that any group of persons, or any one individual, would take the life of a fellow being without some cause. And so, the first important question of this case is, what manner of man was the deceased? Was he a traitor to his country? If he wasn't, I say to the members of this court, then, why did the government fight with all its power, with all the ability, with all the sagacity possessed by them? Every effort on the part of the government was used to keep us from proving that the man was a traitor, and I say in time of war, what charge could be leveled against a human being, a citizen of a country, more reprehensible than to charge him with being a traitor—the only offense described and denounced in the Constitution of the United States. . . . Was he a traitor? As far as America is concerned, he was a German soldier and an enemy to the American government.

"But what happens? When that man was brought to Tonkawa, there came with him the information, and that comes from the intelligence officer, and it was like extracting eyeteeth to get it out, he didn't want to tell it, and it was a struggle that we had to get the information in—when that man Kunze came to Tonkawa, the information came up there with him that there was a man by the name of 'Kun' or something to that effect that wanted to talk. Talk to whom—to the other German prisoners?" Petsch stopped and grimaced at Jaworski, who ignored him. "No, but to the enemies of Germany. What kind of a man do you think would want to communicate with the enemies of his country except a man who was proposing to turn his back on his country? And you remember how difficult it was to prove that first meeting. Not in the middle of September, when he went up there to the hospital, but when they stuck him over there in a barracks, where they went to work and picked up a number of prisoners of war and put them out here in all these barracks when the sergeant put this man Kunze out in a barracks by himself, he signaled the intelligence officer of the Tonkawa Prisoner of War Camp. And when that man came out there, dressed in civilian clothes, and went into those barracks, nobody was in there except Kunze and this civilian, this man who came from the Department of Internal Security of the United States Army at Oklahoma City. Of course, we have no way of finding out what was said. We have no opportunity to be in that building to find out whether or not a conference took place; but is there any man on this court that has any doubt but that conference took place there between Kunze, an enemy of the American government. Is there anybody on this court that is bothered about what they talked about? Is there anybody on this court who believes that Kunze didn't attempt to give information to the enemy at the time? I daresay there is nobody on this court that has any doubt about it.

"That brings up quite a novel proposition of law concerning which you find nothing, I daresay, written in any of the law books in our country. . . ."

Jaworski shook his head and smiled, violating one of his rules that he never showed emotion to what the other side was doing. *Novel.* He wanted the jury to know it was utterly ridiculous.

"I daresay that the situation which occurred in Tonkawa which resulted in the death of Johannes Kunze has never arisen before in the annals of the history of American jurisprudence, and therefore, this is an original case before this court in this respect . . . Here you have a man who proposes to make a traitorous act, who proposes to give information to the enemy. Is it not the duty of every prisoner of war, although he be a prisoner, to do everything within his power to keep his fellow prisoners from aiding the enemy insofar as that aid isn't expressly permitted by the Geneva Convention? Let's reverse the situation; maybe we can then try these accused from their standpoint, as they have to be tried. . . . Suppose we imagine for a moment in a German prisoner of war camp, some American traitor had given information of value, had written it on a piece of paper, that it had been intercepted in its transmission to the German intelligence officers. What do you think the American soldiers would have done? What do you think they should have done? I say, notwithstanding everything that is written, notwithstanding the right and the wrong, in time of war under those conditions, the American soldiers should have done just what the German soldiers have done in this instance—namely, and I believe you will agree with me, take steps to prevent information going to the enemy. I believe that there cannot be any question but that it would be the duty of every American soldier in a prisoner of war camp in Germany or Japan, under the circumstances as we have them here, to do what Sergeant Beyer did—place the matter before the rest of the organization, so they would all know about it.

"If it please the court, one might justly conclude that under circumstances of this kind, when the man was threatening to give further information to the enemy, that these men were even justified, as a matter of law, to take the man's life. Now there isn't anything in the books on it as far as I know, and I believe, with all the exhaustive libraries and the exhaustive study that counsel for the government have made, I don't think they have found anything or will be able to find anything, but that is in this case, that is a matter for your sincere consideration."

Petsch then shifted to an examination of each of the government's three most damaging witnesses. "What did witness Heidutzek testify to? Well, first, let's see what he didn't testify to. He did testify to this: he testified he saw Seidel strike the deceased. He didn't testify that he saw anybody else strike the deceased. He testified that he saw the accused Schomer throw the cups. He didn't testify that Schomer hit the deceased, and he wasn't asked about it. . . . He wasn't asked about it because he knew he hadn't hit him.

"The witness Person gave probably the most damaging testimony because he said that Kunze denied that he wrote the traitorous article. The witness Zorzi didn't know anything damaging to the accused excepting that Beyer told him that he didn't have any business in there and to get out. Oh, I believe the witness Person also testified that he saw the cups thrown, but again he didn't testify that he saw anybody hit anybody with the cups. The inference was once more left with the court that the deceased was seriously injured by the cups being thrown. . . . You remember the scalp wound that the doctor testified was found on the head of the deceased. You will remember on this cup there was no evidence of blood, no hair. Nor was anything shown to this court in connection with that cup except its jagged appearance. Speculation!" he said, hitting the table for emphasis.

"Let me just make this statement to you. It seems to me there can't be any question but when Beyer got this note, this treasonable note, this note written by a traitor—and there can't be any question but what he was a traitor, the evidence is conclusive upon that proposition—when he got the note, what was he to do? What would any soldier have done under the circumstances? A hotheaded soldier might have gone out, after he had convinced himself who the traitor was, and killed the traitor. What did Beyer do? The inference is that he got a group together, and they formulated a design to kill the traitor. Well, if Beyer would have wanted to do that, and you have to judge him as a man of ordinary common sense because the record doesn't disclose that he is a man who doesn't possess ordinary common sense, he certainly would have gone about it in a different manner. He certainly would have gone about it in a different manner than calling a public mass meeting in the night and having the man executed or setting in motion a machine to have him executed under the circumstances as set out here. But what did he do? As a matter of fact, Beyer was faced with this proposition. A man among his men is a traitor to his country. That man is not only trying to give information to the enemy, he has made contact with the enemy. In this note he declares that he wants to give further information to the enemy. Beyer says he believes that if he had done nothing, he would have become a party to the act, or at least he would have become responsible to his government when he got back home for having failed to take action. The United States government seeks to condemn this man because he took action. Now then, did he take action? What kind of action? Did he go out and kill the man? No. He took the matter under advisement and finally called a meeting and made the simple statement of fact that he thought there was a traitor in their company. . . .

"Except the testimony of the accused Schomer, there is no evidence in the record which even to the remotest degree suggests that any one of these accused intended to kill Kunze. Schomer might have had the intention to kill Kunze when he jumped in there, when he came in, jumped on top of the table, grabbed the cups, and started throwing the cups. If he had hit Kunze, the intent to kill would have been presumed, but he didn't hit him. As far as the proof is concerned in this case, there isn't any evidence he ever laid hands on him. Therefore, the intent established by implication of the testimony is immaterial. None of the other defendants, including Beyer, ever hit Kunze. There isn't anything in this record that shows that Beyer ever struck a lick. If it was Beyer's intention that this man was to be killed, as a matter of course, he would have struck the first blow when the deceased came up to examine the paper, but he did not strike him. The government's own witness said that Beyer tried repeatedly to bring the meeting to order and tried to keep the disturbance down, that he tried to stop the affray, the beating which was going on. That is the evidence."

Petsch looked back to Jones to see that he had covered everything, and Jones nodded "yes."

"In conclusion, this responsibility which rests upon my fellow counsel and myself was not a chosen responsibility. It was a responsibility thrust upon us as members of the United States Army, just as the responsibility for trying these men was placed upon your shoulders. We want to perform our part of this responsibility as thoroughly as you gentlemen are going to perform your part when you deliberate this case after the last argument by the government. Whatever the decision may be, there will never be any question in the mind of anyone connected with the defense of this case, but that every member of this court did what his judgment of right directed him to do. Thank you."

Petsch had made some good points. Had it not been wartime and had there been no prisoners of war, his argument might have been excellent mitigation. Who would hang the husband who killed the man who raped his wife? Who would say that American POWs should be executed if they killed a traitor? Tried, yes. But was execution the right answer? Even so, Jaworski felt confident he had convinced the jury it was a death-penalty case.

The jury left the courtroom and did not return for two hours. Colonel Desobry, president of the panel, handed the findings work sheet to Jaworski without saying a word. Jaworski read the result without announcing the findings. It had been agreed that if the jury gave the death penalty, it would not be announced for security reasons.

"The case is closed," Jaworski announced, "and the officers may return to their place of duty." He motioned for the guards to take the condemned men back to their cells. It was five-twenty on January 25, 1944. The trial had taken eight days. Yet it had taken only two hours to seal these men's fate.

Fredrick Opp walked with the five condemned men and their escorts back to the stockade. The moon was bright and illuminated the parade ground so that each man's face appeared ghostly. A drunk American came out of the Officers Club and sang "Chattanooga Choochoo." His good humor disgusted Opp. To hell with all these Americans. What an injustice! These good men should have never even been on trial. It was a matter among Germans and should have been handled by Germans. Opp had tried to inform the Americans that Kunze had committed high treason against the fatherland, but they had ignored him.

The five prisoners had been baffled when no verdict was announced, but Opp had seen the sentencing work sheet. Colonel Petsch had instructed him that the prisoners were not to be told, that they would be informed at a later date once they were out of the camp. But Opp did not feel that was right.

Beyer walked beside Opp. "You seem very upset. What has happened that we should know?"

Opp knew that Beyer had a young wife and son. What would they do without him? "It is not good, my friends."

The other four men cocked their heads to listen.

Petsch had mentioned an appeal. He would tell them about that first. They must have some hope.

"Colonel Petsch says the army must review the sentence before anything can happen. He says that he did not do a very good job, that they should have appointed someone who had experience in criminal law."

"Tell us," Seidel snapped.

The men's breath hung in a cloud over their head; the gravel crunched louder under each step. Finally, Opp told them. "They plan to hang you."

After midnight Beyer heard Hans Demme sobbing in the cell across from his. Demme sat on the floor with his blanket pulled around his shoulders, his blond hair appearing almost white from the moonlight that shone in the barred window.

"Kinder, what is it?" Beyer asked.

Beyer could hear the other men stirring. No one was sleeping tonight.

"It's not fair. This was a matter among Germans," Demme said between sniffles.

Seidel stood and began pacing. "I know why they are doing this. Vengeance. Pure and simple. I heard our guards talking during the trial." He stopped and kicked at his mattress. "All the Americans have had friends killed in the war. This is their way to avenge those deaths."

The talk sounded crazy to Beyer, but who knew anymore. He still could not believe they had been court-martialed for killing a traitor. And the thought they should be hanged seemed the height of insanity.

Beyer watched Demme, the soldier who had seen the fiercest combat among them, as he sobbed into his blanket. He wanted to say something that would sound encouraging, that could offer a glimmer of hope. All Beyer could offer was what he had told his men when they were first captured.

"You are a German, a soldier. Do not forget who you are."

17

Waiting on Death Row

Death Row, Fort Leavenworth, Kansas
1944–1945

THE ARMY'S MAXIMUM SECURITY PRISON, THE UNITED
States Disciplinary Barracks (USDB), consisted of a
large prison yard and limestone buildings surrounded
by a high, thick wall with guard turrets at every
corner. Two thousand prisoners were housed in a
central complex known as "the castle." The structure
was five stories high and was made up of eight
different wings that spoked off a central rotunda. In
the basement of Wing 4, behind a thick steel door was
a bank of twenty cells that served as the German
POWs' death row. There were no windows and naked
bulbs burned day and night. A guard was present
twenty-four hours a day to prevent suicides.

Taking their own lives, however, was the last thing
Beyer and the four other condemned men had on
their minds today. They each had received a thick
bundle of mail from their families and were devour-
ing every page. Beyer smiled broadly at the picture of

211

his Edgar, seated next to a little girl on the lawn in front of his mother's home. He read each letter quickly, then took out a pen and paper to reply.

My Dear Little Wife and Boy:
   It hurts that our boy is asking for his father. From the picture you send, it is clear he will charm all the girls like his daddy. I realize over and over now what a hothead I was when we were together. I can't write what I am thinking about right now . . .

Beyer stopped mid-sentence, recalling Colonel Petsch's visit two months earlier. Sergeant Wilson, the guard on duty that day, had taunted Beyer and the others by saying, "Well, we got some good news and some bad news for you. Your lawyer has come to visit." He put his big hammy fist up to his mouth and snickered. "I guess he'll let you know the bad news," he said opening the thick steel door.

Colonel Petsch, still wearing his top coat, swept in and greeted his five former defendants. He looked much the same with his thinning hair and scarecrow body, arms too long even for his lanky frame. He set his briefcase on the table and came and shook each man's hand. His expression was grave, his handshake a little too firm.

Petsch removed his coat, then took a thick file folder from his briefcase. He cleared his throat and took a deep breath. "I'm sorry to have to tell you men this"—Petsch pressed his lips together tightly, fighting back the emotion—"but you were convicted at trial And the army has sentenced you to be hanged."

Beyer sat stone-faced—old news. As their obnoxious guard had predicted, "bad news," but the shock had worn off.

Petsch waited for an anguished reaction and when he didn't get it he asked, "Do you understand what this means?"

"We knew that night," Beyer said. "Opp told us."

A great burden seemed to have been lifted from Petsch's mind. His grimace disappeared, and he jumped into explaining what he was trying to do. "The good news."

"I wanted to let you know that I just came from Washington, D.C., where I spoke to the Army Board of Review." His brow knitted while he seemed to search for an explanation. "It's an appeals court that could reduce your sentence."

Beyer and the others nodded.

"Anyway, I told them I am just an old country lawyer who had never really handled a court-martial and they should take that into account in the outcome of your trial." Petsch put on a pair of wire-rim reading glasses and opened the file and took out a sheaf of papers. "I wanted to read the last part of the argument I made to them, because I think it might help." He turned over several sheets of paper and began to read.

"There is another matter in this case which is of the utmost importance to the United States government. Under the terms of the Geneva Convention—it is my understanding that I heard it stated in the trial of this case—one copy of this record would be sent to Germany. Of course, when that record gets to Germany and they are advised of the punishment, the Germans will examine the document with the prejudiced attitude that the reviewer naturally would have when advised that five German soldiers had been executed by the United States government attempting to prevent a man from committing further traitorous acts against Germany. You know that that reviewer is bound to be prejudiced. And I will say that when he reads this record, he is very apt to conclude, although without justification, that these men were executed not for the purpose of protecting other German prisoners of war against murder from their fellow prisoners but were executed solely because they were German prisoners. . . ."

Seidel glanced at Beyer, and they both raised their eyebrows in agreement. They had discussed their sentence often and decided that vengeance was the only reason the Americans could justify hanging them.

Petsch read on: ". . . And if that should be his report to the German authorities, then the German government, if they believed and agreed with the reviewer, would have no recourse other than to pay in kind whenever a similar opportunity arose. I believe it is a question of utmost importance, because I am sure that no group of American officers could be found—I will say I am sure—who would say that similar acts on the part of American soldiers under identical or similar circumstances committed in a German prisoner of war camp could be reprehensible to the extent of justifying the execution of five American soldiers, even if they had been proved guilty."

Petsch took off his glasses. "I can't guarantee you anything, but I felt like I was getting through to them. It's not fair. We would have expected the same thing from our POWs."

As Petsch was leaving, Beyer and the other men had thanked him for all he had done, but the condemned men had not been optimistic. Nine other German POWs had been sentenced to death and were at the USDB for killing traitors in Arkansas and Arizona. The Americans were not going to listen to any defenses. Beyer and the others were Germans, and the Americans hated everything German.

When the notice had come from the Board of Review at the end of April that their sentences had been upheld, Beyer had not been surprised.

He returned to his letter, looking for something positive he could say to Edith:

I cannot help the tone of my letters. Just know that my love for you grows stronger and stronger. The guards play music that sounds like howling wolves to me. I long to hear classical music: Wagner and Verdi. All love to the boy and a thousand kisses.

Better to stop there. If Edith knew his true predicament, it would just cause her more heartache.

Swiss Embassy, Washington, D.C.
April 1945

Werner Weingaertner, Chief of German Interests of the Swiss Legation, sat behind his large oak desk and read the cablegram he had just received from the German embassy in Bern. He was a small man in his mid-thirties with a broad mustache and thinning brown hair. Weingaertner prided himself on getting along with both sides in this conflict. The message announced that the German government would not execute fifteen American POWs if the United States would exchange fifteen German POWs under death sentence.

"Thank God," he said out loud.

Ambassador Charles Bruggmann would be pleased. Since January the Swiss embassy had been embroiled in this contest of wills. The American president had already signed the death warrants on five German POWs, but then postponed the executions until May 1 because of the German threat of retaliation. Finally, it seemed as though both sides were going to solve this matter without deaths.

Werner knocked on Bruggmann's door and asked to have a word with him. The ambassador was a large man with brown hair and washed-out blue eyes. In his early fifties, Bruggmann was one of the most respected diplomats in the Swiss Corps. He motioned Weingaertner into his office. The room was redolent with the smell of freshly cut lilacs from the embassy garden.

"Werner, please tell me it is good news?"

Weingaertner read the cable. "The Third Reich is prepared to exchange fifteen American prisoners of war under sentence of death for an equal number of Germans under sentence of death. The Third Reich further agrees to postpone for the duration of the exchange negotiations the date of execution already imposed on the American prisoners of war."

Bruggmann sat with his hands steepled in front of his face for a long time. At last, he said, "I spoke with the American State Department today. They would like us to arrange the exchange." He rubbed the back of his neck, then rotated his head from side to side. With the Nazi's defeat near and refugees streaming out of Germany, the borders were a mess. Any exchange would be plagued with problems. "They will transport the German POWs to the Swiss-French frontier, and the Germans are to bring the condemned Americans to the German-Swiss border for a joint exchange. You've done well, Werner."

Weingaertner felt relieved. He had witnessed the trial in Oklahoma and felt that the sentence had been too harsh for the circumstances. The killing was done in the heat of the moment; the victim was a traitor. This was not the kind of case that warranted capital punishment.

The ambassador made a note on his calendar. "The Americans have agreed to postpone any execution until May first. They are concerned that the war is almost over, and they may not be able to get their men out. We need to move on this *very, very* quickly."

Death Row, Fort Leavenworth, Kansas
April–May 1945

Beyer was finishing a book by Jack London about Alaska, when the heavy steel door to death row swung open and a man in civilian clothes walked through. For a moment the man looked like his brother, Karl. It cannot be, he thought. My mind is going; this must be a hallucination. But quickly enough he heard his brother's voice.

"Little brother," Karl shouted good-naturedly, then rushed and shook Beyer's hand. The guard unlocked the cell and let in Karl. He bear-hugged Beyer.

It was Karl! How was it possible?

As overjoyed as he was to see his brother, Beyer pulled back and whispered, "How did you get in? You are a German. The war is still on." Beyer feared the guards might arrest Karl on the spot.

Karl seemed unconcerned and brushed the idea away by saying that he was married to an American. He was a thicker-set version of Beyer, but without the temper. They both had the same dark brown hair and striking blue eyes. Karl had left Germany long ago to first work in the oil fields in Mexico and now at an air force base in Mississippi. Beyer had never figured out why the Americans had allowed his brother to stay in this country. Karl always seemed to have the luck his brother was denied.

Karl sat on the bunk and motioned for Beyer to do the same. "They have not given me much time. I have written to the provost marshal in Washington." Karl paused to make sure his brother understood the importance of what he had been doing. "He believes that if you would provide the names of the others involved in the killing of Kunze, they would reduce your sentence."

Beyer drew back. "Did the Americans ask you to do this?"

Perhaps that explained why they had let Karl stay in this country. Nothing surprised Beyer anymore.

A shadow of pain spread over Karl's face. "No, brother," he said sadly.

Beyer felt terrible for suspecting the worst from a family member. "I'm sorry. It is just that I am under a great deal of pressure."

Karl nodded that he understood.

"I cannot give other names. The Americans are sure I know more, but I'm not sure of the other people. If I were to give other men's names they would end up here like me, and I would have to eventually look their families in the eyes for what I had done. I might be tried once I got home."

Karl drew back, his mouth slacked open. "Have you not seen what has been coming out of the homeland?" Karl shouted. "The army is the one who will be tried!"

Several prisoners looked up from playing dominoes. Beyer nodded that he was fine. Beyer knew from what the Catholic priest, Chaplain Towle, had told them that Germany was losing the war and it might be over soon. Other than that, Beyer did not understand what his brother meant.

"The camps," Karl whispered. When this did not

register, he said, "Concentration camps. Thousands of Jews murdered. The Americans hate us now." Karl opened his eyes wide and nodded his head emphatically. "I hear it every day."

Beyer did not understand what this had to do with him. Yes, he had seen the camps, but knew nothing about the murder of Jews. He had never been a Nazi or believed in any of their racism. His own mother had helped a Jewish dentist and his family escape from Hamburg.

"Karl, I'm a soldier. I had nothing to do with that."

Karl closed his eyes and sighed heavily. "You do not understand what the mood is like in this country. They want to punish us. Surely you must know someone else who took part in the killing."

Beyer sat in silence staring at his bed. His brother meant well, but Beyer would not break the code he lived by. To do so would make him no better than the traitor Kunze. "No," he said, "I won't do that to my men."

Karl looked at his watch. "I was told that the Swiss government is working on a prisoner of war swap."

Beyer looked up, he eyes teary. "It's the reason we have not been executed. Without that hope, I don't know if I could keep going."

Then it was time for Karl to leave. The guard searched both Beyer and Karl, to make sure nothing had been smuggled. Beyer hugged him one more time, then said, "If anything happens, make sure Edith knows."

Karl walked toward the large steel door, then

turned and looked once more at Beyer. All through their visit Karl had remained dry-eyed, but now he was sobbing. He looked piteously at Beyer.

"Don't feel sorry for me, brother. I am doing what is right."

USDB, Fort Leavenworth, Kansas
May 1945

It was the cheering that woke Beyer from his morning nap. He glanced up and saw Chaplain Towle walking briskly toward their cells. The noise was coming from the other wings of the prison. Loud clapping and yelling.

"Father, what is it?" asked Seidel.

Towle, a short man with kind brown eyes and a long nose, was the Roman Catholic chaplain at Fort Leavenworth. He spoke fluent German and had befriended the POWs on death row. He motioned for the men to sit down at the wooden tables and chairs that had been provided outside their cells and waited until they were quiet.

"Hitler has killed himself in Berlin. They found him outside his bunker . . ."

Simultaneously, the men fired questions at Towle "Was the war over? What would happen to them now? Was it the Russians who captured Berlin? Would the new American president, Truman, look at their cases again?" Beyer sat up on his bunk and rubbed the sleep from his eyes.

Towle raised his hand for silence. "It just came over

the radio. Germany has unconditionally surrendered. The Russians and the U.S. captured Berlin."

Beyer watched his men's faces sadden. All they had fought for was in vain. Their country was destroyed. Surely, the Americans could not want to kill them now. The war was over. Beyer prayed that Russians were not overrunning Hamburg.

"What will happen to us?" Seidel asked again.

Towle's lips pressed into a thin line as he held up his hands in exasperation. "Fellows, I just don't know. I have told you what I know." The priest caught Beyer's eye, who was still seated in his cell. He looked concerned, too unhappy for this announcement.

He knows something.

Then it tumbled into Beyer's mind. The American POWs who were to be swapped. How would they be exchanged if there was no government? Maybe they were dead? There was no way an exchange could take place.

Beyer rose from his bunk and stood in the cell doorway. He waited for a break in his men's questions, then asked, "Father, the exchange?"

Towle would only meet Beyer's gaze for a second before he turned away. "I wish I knew."

Washington, D.C.
May 1945

Weingaertner decided to take a long walk along the Potomac instead of eating lunch. Though it was a sunny day, a harsh wind churned up whitecaps on the river, and cherry blossoms littered the sidewalk. The negotiations for the POW release were unraveling. Hitler had killed himself on April 30. There was no one in Berlin who could assure Truman that the American POWs would be delivered to the Swiss border. Weingaertner had read the cables from Bern this morning. The plan was to do nothing and not attempt to deliver the American proposal, hoping that both sides would continue their pledges not to execute prisoners until they heard from the other side. Inaction was always part of diplomacy, but Weingaertner was not so sure it would hold with Germany a vanquished enemy.

He turned up the collar of his suit coat and faced the water, watching the waves slam into the bridge pylons. There would be pressure to punish anything connected with Germany now. Pictures of the concentration camps were filtering back to the United States and being printed in magazines. Horrible! Millions murdered; human beings stacked up like cord wood. The public would want someone to pay. Weingaertner suspected these five POWs would be the first of many to head to the gallows.

The Oval Office, Washington, D.C.
July 2, 1945

A gentle morning light shone through the double French doors of the Oval Office, as President Harry Truman sat behind his desk reviewing the file on five German POWs awaiting execution at Fort Leavenworth. Truman was in a sour mood. His wife, Bess, and daughter, Margaret, had taken the train back to

Independence, making it clear they did not care for the new demands the presidency made on his time. Already he missed their company, their hounding him about his loud ties, his haircut, his shoes. Two months earlier he had been completely happy being Vice President. With the death of Roosevelt, his life had been turned upside down. He prayed it did not destroy his family.

Henry Stimson, the Secretary of War, sat silently in the wicker-backed chair next to Truman's desk as the president read a description of the crime. Nazi thugs had murdered one of their own. They had been given a fair trial with two lawyers defending them. The Army Board of Review confirmed their sentence. The one thing that gave Truman reason for pause was the communiqué saying American POWs were being held under a death sentence and would be executed if we hanged these five Germans.

Blackmail.

After what those Nazi bastards did at Dachau and Bergen-Belsen, they had no right to bargain for anything.

Truman turned his fat leather chair toward Stimson. "Henry, are you absolutely sure we've got our fifteen boys back?"

Stimson was a Roosevelt man, a Yalie full of waspish pretension, but Truman respected him and his judgment. "Mr. President," Stimson said in his clipped tone, "all our men have been recovered. All of them were in POW camps that have been liberated."

Truman picked up the pen and prepared to sign the order authorizing the execution, then stopped. "Are the Swiss going to cause us any trouble on this?" His eyes looked larger than life behind his wire-rim glasses.

"I've been told they never sent our last offer to exchange prisoners because they knew the Nazis couldn't comply. For all the world knows, we never made the offer. The Swiss have nothing to gain by causing a problem."

"Good." Truman signed the order with a flare. "We can't appear to be weak to Uncle Joe." He was scheduled to meet with Stalin and Churchill at Potsdam in two weeks. Too much was at stake in Europe now for foreign leaders to misjudge America's resolve because she had a new president.

Stimson retrieved the order.

"I want a progress report from Oppenheimer on the S-1 project before we head overseas."

It had taken less than five minutes to dispose of the problem. Truman had larger issues on his mind. An invasion of Japan might cost a million U.S. lives. His experts were unsure whether they could perfect this new weapon called the atom bomb in time for it to be of any use in the war. Russia was eager to gobble up half of Europe if the U.S. gave it a chance. None of these problems would be as easy as the one he had just dealt with.

18

The Execution

USDB, Fort Leavenworth, Kansas
July 8, 1945

WALTER BEYER STOOD AT HIS CELL DOOR TALKING TO Seidel, both of them still optimistic about their fate after what had happened two days earlier with Sergeant Edgar Menschner. On that morning a lieutenant and two guards had appeared and told Menschner that his sentence had been commuted to twenty years and that he was moving upstairs to the general prison population. Menschner had killed a fellow POW who was merely volunteering to do work for the Americans, one whom he had not even been sure was a spy. Seidel said that if they were showing mercy to Menschner, their cases were even more compelling. The war was over, there could not be a reason to kill them anymore.

But an hour later, the commandant of the USDB, Colonel Eley, marched into death row, flanked by two chaplains. The guards ordered the men to attention and Colonel Eley read from a set of orders: "General Court-Martial Order Number 262: Charge I: Viola-

226

tion of the 92nd Article of War. Specification: In that Walter Beyer, Berthold Seidel, Hans Demme, Hans Schomer, and Willi Scholz, all being prisoners of war in the Prisoner of War Camp, Tonkawa, Oklahoma, acting jointly and in pursuance of common intent, did, at the Prisoner of War Camp, Tonkawa, Oklahoma, on or about November 4, 1943, with malice aforethought, willfully, deliberately, feloniously, unlawfully, and with premeditation, kill one Johannes Kunze, a human being, by striking him with their fists and with instruments not known." Colonel Eley took a long breath and waited for the interpreter to finish. "Charge II: Violation of the 89th Article of War. Specification: In that Walter Beyer, Berthold Seidel, Hans Demme, Hans Schomer, and Willi Scholz, being prisoners of war and in camp at the Prisoner of War Camp, Tonkawa, Oklahoma, did at Prisoner of War Camp, Tonkawa, Oklahoma on or about November 4, 1943, commit a riot, in that they together with certain other prisoners of war to the number of twenty or more, and whose names are unknown, did unlawfully and riotously and in a violent and tumultuous manner, assemble to disturb the peace of said camp, and having so assembled, did unlawfully and riotously assault Johannes Kunze, to the terror and disturbance of the said Johannes Kunze.

"Pleas to the specification and charge by each accused: Not guilty.

"Findings of the specifications and charges as to each accused: Guilty.

"Sentence as to each accused: To be hanged by the neck until dead."

Beyer found it hard to breathe. His heart raced as if he had just run kilometers.

Colonel Eley placed this order in a folder and took out a different piece of paper and continued: "The sentence having been approved by the reviewing authority, the record of trial forwarded for the action of the President, and the record of trial having been examined by the Board of Review in the judge advocate general's office; and the Board of Review having submitted its opinion in writing to the judge advocate general, and the record of trial, the opinion of the Board of Review, and the recommendations of the judge advocate general having been transmitted directly to the secretary of war for the action of the President, and having been laid before the President, the following are his orders thereon: 'In the foregoing case of German prisoners of war Walter Beyer, Berthold Seidel, Hans Demme, Hans Schomer, Willi Scholz, the sentence of each accused is confirmed and will be carried into executions under the direction of the commandant. Said executions are to take place between the hours of 0001 and 0600, Central War Time, on July 10, 1945.'"

Colonel Eley replaced the orders in his file, did a sharp about-face, and marched out. The guard yelled, "at ease," and Beyer stumbled back to his bunk and collapsed. This could not be happening, not when the war was over. What was the point in killing them? The words of the fortune-teller so long ago swarmed at him: "Don't go across the sea, there is danger for you." What would his Edith do? How would his little prince survive without his father?

228

"Damn bastard," Seidel muttered in the next cell. "They had agreed to exchange Americans who did the same thing. How can they go back on that promise? Isn't it enough that they have destroyed Germany?"

Beyer closed his eyes, trying to keep the tears back. He had no answer for Seidel.

None of the men slept that night, and Beyer was up early working on a letter to his wife. He had thought all night about what to say. More than anything he wanted Edgar to have a letter telling him that his father had done no wrong. He wrote:

My Edith, who I love above anyone else:

By the time you receive this I will be called to the big "Army" in the sky. I have thought about what I did and before myself and God, I can say I've gone over everything and I am not guilty. I can only tell you this is being done because of hatred against all that is German. I love you with all the power of my heart. I will love you till death tells all. Raise our son to be a good German. Tell him not to be ashamed of his father. Don't run yourself down trying to give our son a good education. I have prepared a last will and testament. I hope you will receive a signet wedding ring and wristwatch that belong to me. Thank you for every hour by your side. You will need to be a leader and guide to our son. Do it with pride. He must grow up without a father now. Good-bye. May fate be good to you. Don't ever forget me. A thousand kisses to you and our son.

Love,
Walter

Tears ran down his face and stained the letter. Beyer could think of nothing more to say or do. Rather than dwell on the letter any longer, he tried to relive every pleasant moment he had with his wife and son. He tried to imagine just once more the smell of the ocean in Hamburg. After a few minutes it came to him, and he felt that same joy he received watching a big freighter sail out of the harbor into the sea, the clouds white and billowy on the horizon, until finally the ship, no bigger than a sliver, disappeared forever.

Just before midnight, Beyer heard the dull thud of boots marching down the hall, then the large steel door banged opened and a lieutenant led a detail of six guards with rifles. The lieutenant stopped in front of his cell and announced, "Walter Beyer." A guard came around and opened the cell with his key. Beyer, dressed in his gray Afrika Korps tunic and hat, was allowed to shake hands with the four other condemned men.

At Seidel's cell, Beyer said, "Someday they will see that this is wrong."

Seidel swallowed hard, fighting back tears. "We did what any good soldier would have done."

With that the guard tapped Beyer's shoulder and the detail—Beyer surrounded on all sides by armed guards—marched out of death row, up a flight of stairs, and into the summer night. The heat surprised Beyer, hitting him in the face like a slap. The night was full of noise, crickets, cicadas; the air was full and rich with the smell of summer. The stars seemed bright enough to blind him. So many things he had forgotten. Silently, Beyer said the Twenty-third Psalm to himself. "Yea though I walk through the valley of the shadow of death, I shall fear no evil."

The guards were taking him to some type of warehouse about a quarter of a kilometer from the castle. White light poured out of the door and down a huge wooden ramp. Beyer marched inside, and the light seemed even brighter. There were guards along the wall, some civilians, and Colonel Eley. They marched Beyer up to a wooden platform with a large black circle painted on it. A noose hung from a beam overhead.

"For the Lord is my shepherd."

"Attention," Colonel Eley commanded, bringing the entire room to silence. "First Sergeant Walter Beyer, having been convicted of murder, you are to be hanged by the neck until dead." It was the same order he had read from a day earlier. "Do you have anything to say?"

"I cannot understand why this should be done to me."

Colonel Eley motioned for the sergeant standing behind Beyer to remove his hat and replace it with a black hood. The noose was fitted over Beyer's head and tightened around his neck. It was a simple, but efficient gallows: workers had built a wooden platform with a trapdoor over an elevator shaft. The noose hung from a beam on the second floor. The body would drop down the shaft into the basement. After the execution, the platform could be removed so the elevator could be put back into operation.

Edith and Edgar, I will always love you!

Eley held his hand up and said, "May God have mercy on your soul!" With a quick downward jab of his hand, Eley motioned for the sergeant to release the lever on the trapdoor.

The trapdoor grated open, and Walter Beyer hurtled toward the basement, the rope bouncing slightly as his weight took up the slack.

In the basement Major Roy Cram, the fort surgeon, watched emotionlessly as Beyer's body twitched and convulsed above him. Urine ran down Beyer's legs and dripped onto the floor. A stepladder had been provided and every five minutes, Doctor Cram would climb the steps and listen for a heartbeat.

Chaplain Towle said a prayer as he watched, his face etched with concern.

"Don't worry, Father," Major Cram said, "he isn't feeling a thing."

Twenty minutes later, Walter Beyer was dead.

The next morning Colonel Eley and two chaplains accompanied the bodies to the convict graveyard on a wooded hill overlooking the USDB. Bill Ratford, a newspaperman from the *Kansas City Star* who had been permitted to watch the hanging, accompanied the burial party. He had filed his piece on the hanging this morning under the lead: "Five Nazi POWS Hanged For Killing NAZI FOE." He had liked the piece. Good description of Beyer, "Black stubble, matching his hair. His eyes those of a trapped beast." And he especially liked the end where he tied up the entire war: "In an Oklahoma prisoner of war camp, on Nov. 4, 1943, they beat to death a fellow prisoner of war who had committed treason, in their opinion, by losing faith in Adolf Hitler and the Nazi ideology." But now he was looking for a short follow-up piece. Maybe something about how the army buried people.

Ratford stood next to Colonel Eley and watched as they lowered the wooden caskets into the graves, and the chaplain said a short word for each man's soul. The mosquitoes were out and taking a piece out of his neck.

"Whose are these other graves?" Ratford asked, pointing at four rows of white markers near the fence.

"Soldiers who were executed or died at the DB and their folks or relatives didn't want the bodies."

Ratford took out his reporter's notebook and scribbled down a note about this. Not enough for a story, he thought.

Then Eley volunteered, "They used to be buried down in the post cemetery, but Washington found out and raised hell. Said men who died in dishonor shouldn't be buried with other veterans. So they moved them up here in"—Eley swatted at a bug on his arm—"must have been 1911. Plus, they had the headstones turned West. The ones down in the other cemetery face north."

"Why's that?" Ratford asked.

Eley was a big man with a balding head. He was sweating through his khakis and seemed ready to get out of the sun. "It's a sign of military dishonor. When Gabriel sounds the trumpet for the resurrection in the east, these souls won't hear it and will be left behind." He raised his hands and shrugged, as if to say who knows.

Ratford nodded. He liked it. Godless, atheistic Nazis' souls left behind on Judgment Day. Where was their almighty Hitler now? He scribbled a few more notes. If he didn't get a story out about it, they could run it as an editorial. *Their souls were left behind.* That was real justice.

Hamburg, Germany
August 2, 1946

Edith Beyer was cooking beans in the backyard of her parents' home, where she and her five-year-old son, Edgar, lived. The day was hot, the sky full of big gray clouds that meant evening rain. She wore a plain housedress, and her brown hair was pulled back and pinned to her head. When Walter was home, she worked so hard to look beautiful for him. But now those sorts of worries seemed silly. The winter had been so hard. So little food, the city in rubble, and no word about Walter. Still, she was better off than most. She'd found a job as a secretary. The money was enough to buy a scrap of meat for the potatoes once a week. And above all else she had their little prince, Edgar.

She stopped stirring the pot and watched him play with a ball in the grass near the back steps. He was a good-natured boy, and he had grown so much. Walter would not recognize him.

A half hour later Edith heard the postman's bell. She laid down her ladle and hurried to the front driveway. Each day held out the possibility of hearing from her Walter. One of her neighbors had just recently received word that her husband was in a forced labor camp in Russia. Edith knew they would never allow that in America. The delay in hearing from him was more likely a breakdown in the postal service in Germany. The postman handed her a single postcard and quickly walked to the next house. Edith carried the card back to where she was canning. She had hoped it was a letter from Walter. It was some kind of announcement from the government. They had been receiving notices monthly about everything from meat rationing to curfew. Then she read the card.

"Oh, my God," she screamed. The postcard said that Walter had died in America. Shot. It would be another year before she would find out the real facts: Walter had been hanged for murder.

Edith's whole body began to shake, and she let out a piercing wail. Edgar ran to his mother and hugged at her legs.

"Mutti, Mutti, what is it?" he asked.

But she did not hear him.

For ten minutes she wailed as though she were an animal being slaughtered.

Epilogue

Fort Leavenworth, Kansas
March 1990

EDGAR BEYER STOOD IN FRONT OF A SIMPLE WHITE tombstone that marked his father's grave in the U.S. Disciplinary Barracks Cemetery. He was a successful Hamburg banker, forty-eight years old, with a broad face and wavy salt-and-pepper hair that he inherited from his mother. His visit here ten years earlier had left him feeling hollow and angry. Time had not changed his grief much. He wept silently as he bent down and touched the marker.

Walter
Beyer
—
Hauptfeldwebel
German
July 10, 1945

His family had never been very open about his father's death during World War II, especially his

237

mother. She had waited until Edgar was ready to marry before she informed him that Walter had been hanged for murder and was buried in a convict graveyard. After his first visit, Edgar made it a point to obtain a copy of the record of trial and read every word. It was clear that his father had done no wrong. Walter had acted as any good soldier would have when he discovered a traitor in his midst.

The graveyard looked different than it had ten years earlier. Plastic flowers had been placed in front of each grave, and someone had scrubbed the grime off the white granite stones so they gleamed. John Reichley, a fort historian, had told Edgar that post officials believed that it had been done by the wife of a German officer attending the Command and General Staff College, but that no one knew for sure.

Beyer kissed the gravestone, then said a silent prayer. His wife, Marianne, stood by his side and held his hand. The life they had made in Germany was so much better and different than their parents'. The two boys they had brought into the world would hopefully never have to face a world war.

"I wish your mother had seen the grave before she died," Marianne said.

After a long silence, Edgar said, "Too bitter."

A group of Afrika Korps veterans had recently contacted Edgar about bringing his father's remains home and giving him a hero's burial in a German military cemetery. Though Edgar had given the idea some thought, this visit convinced him otherwise. The grave served as a reminder of what had been done during the war, what zealousness could cause a people to do in the name of justice.

Below the wooded hill, the muddy Missouri River pushed toward the Mississippi. A large evergreen shaded most of the graves, and mourning doves sang in the nearby woods. Peaceful countryside, thought Edgar, much like the area of Schleswig-Holstein in Germany. It was a good place for his father to rest.